# ENDORS

"In *Lessons from the Edge*, Vaughn shares his insightful and intense journey of working to bring his company back from the edge. With humility and an engaging style, he treats the reader to a lifetime of business lessons, essential reading for any leader who hopes to propel their business back into forward motion after a setback. This book is an MBA course of practical steps from someone who has been there and is a go-to guide for making the right decisions in difficult times. Vaughn keeps the reader engaged as he transparently shares what he learned and how he came back from the edge of disaster to find both success and significance. Well Done!"
— Ken Gosnell, Founder and Chief Experience Officer: CXP, Author of *Well Done*

"You need to read this book if...

- You are just starting or thinking about starting a business.
- You have already started your business and find it in crisis.
- You have your own business but feel stuck and want to get it growing again.

A quick review of the chapter titles in the table of contents will show you the lessons this book covers. Trust me, you'll need this "How-to and How NOT to" information as an aid to your business progress. Study these lessons well and enhance your chance for entrepreneurial success."
— Al Slade, Radio personality, Founder, Slade & Associates, Lifelong sales innovator

"This book is both raw and powerful. For leaders under pressure, the honesty and perspective in this book are refreshing and immediately helpful. I truly found myself drawn into the lessons on preparing for and responding to crisis and the seventeen takeaways to turnaround. This book will make a difference for those who read it. Vaughn's humility is disarming, exposing the reader to poignant lessons that draw them into honest self-reflection, unlocking the potential for personal growth."

—Jon Switzer, Founder, Crossed Bridges

# lessons from the
# EDGE
## of business disaster

A Leader's Guide to **Survival** and **Recovery**

## VAUGHN C. THURMAN

WITH CHUCK TRESSLER

FREILING
PUBLISHING

Published by Freiling Publishing, a division of Freiling Agency, LLC.

P.O. Box 1264
Warrenton, VA 20188

www.FreilingPublishing.com

PB ISBN: 978-1-956267-44-0
e-Book ISBN: 978-1-956267-45-7

*Printed in the United States of America*

# DEDICATION

I dedicate this book to my tireless wife, Betsy, who has endured much on the way to the present and yet helped me feel God's undeserved love, and to my children, who helped me laugh and see what matters.

# TABLE OF CONTENTS

# INTRODUCTION

My passion and purpose for this book are to discuss what I learned as I reached the tipping point of entrepreneurial failure. I confronted a situation that would strike fear in the hearts of even the bravest of entrepreneurs. I wish someone had warned me, and I wish the cure had been as simple as having someone grab my chair as it was about to tip and prevent all of it from happening. Perhaps they could have warned me more specifically, "I've walked through that dark room you are about to enter and stubbed my toes really badly. There's an enormous piece of furniture right in the middle of the room, so look out for it!"

The truth is I had to learn the hard way. But for the grace of God and the lessons I learned at a high cost, I should not have survived. It has not been easy to be transparent about when everything went wrong and how I was the one responsible. Still, for the benefit of others, I have decided to share my story of going to the verge of bankruptcy and how I survived and executed a turnaround professionally, personally, and financially. I went from standing at the edge of a cliff convinced I would fall to seeing significant success, but the course correction did not begin until I was humbled enough to ask for help.

Now it is my turn to offer what I wish someone had been able to offer me. I'm going to tell you about the furniture in that dark room of entrepreneurship. If that helps just one fellow entrepreneur who may be struggling alone, then sharing my story of near disaster and the slow and painful recovery will be worth it.

# LESSON #1

# "THE TRUTH WILL SET YOU FREE"

Colonel Nathan R. Jessup, Jack Nicholson's character in the movie *A Few Good Men*, provided one of the most memorable lines in contemporary cinema.

Misguided as it may have been in this situation, my "Colonel Nathan R. Jessup" moment had arrived as I barked out to my mother-in-law: "The truth? You can't handle the truth!"

It was a conversation I did not want to have, especially with my mother-in-law. Knowing full well that something was wrong, she insisted that I had to confide in someone. It was my son's seventh birthday, and I just wanted to pretend to be a normal husband, father, and family man and to act as if everything was all right. As I found myself overwhelmed by fear and other emotions that I couldn't hide, I tried to escape from my son's birthday party for a moment by taking out the trash. It was unnerving and surreal to find that my mother-in-law was on to me and had pursued me outside to the trash bins. I felt as if my life had turned into an episode of *The Twilight Zone*, and here I was in that middle ground between light and shadow.

"You want to know what's going on?" I continued, just as overzealously as before. "You want to know what I'm dealing with? Do you really?"

1

My brother-in-law sarcastically describes my mother-in-law as a woman who "has an answer for everything." He pokes fun at her, in good spirit, for always having a specific prescription for everyone's maladies. If you say you feel tired, she might say, "You should go walk around the house three times," to which he would immediately chime in, "Are you sure three and half times wouldn't be better?" leading them both to chuckle. I sometimes have trouble getting along with her because I typically have a different answer for everything, but not this time. I had no answers at all.

"You have to tell me what's going on," she continued. "You have to have someone to talk to. Trust me. You will feel better!"

I finally caved. "The bank sent me a letter a little over a week ago and I need at least a hundred and seventy-five thousand dollars and I've got about seventeen days left to come up with the money or they're coming for the house!" I finally confessed, the words spilling out in a stream without punctuation except for the exclamation point at the end, as I turned so abruptly on my pursuer that she crashed into me.

"What will you do?" she asked, the once confident, all-knowing look gone from her face.

After mumbling something about having little more than the overdue mortgage payment with which to battle this dragon, I added more coherently, "And we may all have to move into your basement." I was not being sarcastic, although my response was laced with sarcasm.

The color was now vanishing from her face. I was sure that I heard her gulp.

### *"But wait ... there's more!"*

Now it was my turn to be relentless, so I answered just a bit too intensely while channeling my inner Ron Popeil, who endlessly pitched Ronco Products on TV throughout the 70s and 80s, or perhaps it was Billy Mays in the 90s extolling the virtues of Oxi Clean.

"But wait—there's more! It gets better! The IRS showed up at my office a couple of days ago, and now I'm not sure that I would be moving into your basement with Betsy and the kids if it comes to that."

My mother-in-law was right. I did feel better. I felt a whole lot better! But it had nothing to do with unburdening myself. I'm ashamed to admit that it was because my all-knowing mother-in-law had become speechless for the first time ... ever.

Well, here's the good news. We made it through all of this and probably never would have without a great deal of help from my mother-in-law, who often came to help my wife paint rooms or rearrange furniture or the many other things I couldn't do because I was always at work. And in the end, by God's grace, I've pulled it off and lived up to the age-old adage that behind every successful man ... is an astounded mother-in-law!

### I waited too long to address the obvious

I came to realize that there was a great deal of wisdom in Colonel Jessop's words. His outburst expressed something authentic. Most of us cannot "handle the truth." That is why many of our problems in life come from our avoidance or denial of life's more difficult realities. In his book *Good to Great*, Jim Collins calls them "the brutal facts," and I certainly avoided plenty of those to get to the edge. I suddenly realized that while thoroughly convinced of my mother-in-law's inability to handle the truth, the brutal fact was that I was the one who needed to face the reality that I had for far too long wished away. I had been living in denial and not at all successfully.

> *Life is less complicated and stressful*
> *when we choose to face the truth, no matter how*
> *unpleasant, ugly, or brutal it may be.*

Thank God, this is NOT the end of my story. It ends better than you might expect with favorable turnarounds in numerous areas. I went from having a failing business to a succeeding business, but it took a lot of work, patience, and good fortune combined with a healthy dose of divine providence. By 2012, after going sideways in business for more than half a decade, I finally recognized the need to change practically everything about the way I conducted business and my personal life. By 2015, I had begun to develop multi-year plans to turn the business around and to reinvest in myself through weight loss, learning, and restoring broken relationships. I also had to learn to say "no" to various things so that I would have the room to focus on what I needed to say "yes" to.

By 2018, the obvious or expected outcome of the disaster I will describe to you in this book had not only been avoided, but I also had gotten the business to the point where it was growing by 35 percent a year, increasing in value, and turning an increasingly healthy profit, and that part of my story ended with a sale of a successful business for many millions of dollars. I had gone from rags (as a kid with big dreams) to riches (as a young entrepreneur with big debts) back to rags (a failing entrepreneur with a big disaster, including all that debt) to real wealth. As all of this transpired, I had become an experienced businessperson the old-fashioned way, i.e., I got my degree at the school of hard knocks. I believe I survived these errors not so that I could brag to you about surviving or what I accomplished. Rather, I think the reason I survived was so that I could share these lessons learned with others who find themselves in what may seem to be impossible circumstances.

As I navigated from being a spectacle of impending disaster (i.e., the leader of a local business that for years was rumored as being about to fail) to a surprising success, I began to expose my ugly story to others, hoping to draw them in so that I could also openly share the lessons I had learned along the way. At one point, I coalesced the lessons into a presentation called "Lessons from the Edge," which eventually became the basis for this book. I delivered that presentation in front of numerous and varied audiences. A common occurrence after delivering my presentation was having entrepreneurs who had previously known only about my successes approach me to share their own stories of crisis in business. Many of them had previously not shared this truth with anyone. After all, who wants to go around saying, "Hi, my name is Jack, and my business is failing"? But in the absence of such soul-cleansing truth, imagine the isolation that secrecy brings on so many entrepreneurs!

Being able to tell people the specifics of my errors and how I learned to recover from them in practical ways was a real joy for me. I love helping people connect to both reality and hope. My disaster had become my calling card to help people find success, and it was made more credible by the fact that I had taken my own well-known mess and turned it into something that others eventually wanted to buy.

Getting to this very different outcome involved replacing *hard* work with *smart* work. I had to replace employees who were easy to manage with professionals who were often difficult to manage because they thought they saw a better way to do things. I was in trouble, and I didn't need fans—I needed workers. I needed smart workers. I needed to learn to stop making excuses and start focusing on forward progress. I had to stop seeing problems as being "outside the building," where I believed I was a victim of something beyond my control. I needed to start addressing the real problems that were most often "inside the building" and very often rooted in my own deficient behaviors as a leader. I'm going to be very transparent throughout the rest of this book as I share both the error of my ways and the significant costs of those errors, as well as what I learned and how I survived, recovered, and eventually overcame these many obstacles of my own making.

Throughout the course of this book, I will share that many of these obstacles had to do with my own thinking. I thought more money would solve all my problems. It would not have done anything remotely like that. Throwing more money at a broken system doesn't make it better; it makes it more expensive, and it prolongs the inevitable collapse. My journey had to start in the mind and in the heart, and when change began there—surprise, surprise!—the money situation seemed to improve as well. If only a few politicians might feel inclined to read this book!

While success has its benefits, I would not desire to have achieved mine by skipping these lessons. Many of these lessons were learned during the darkest days of this story, and they are precious to me, lessons I could not have learned any other way.

### Humility and the willingness to change

First, I had to take an honest look at myself. I had to get out of my own way! I had to face the brutal truths about myself and be willing to change.

What leads us to become entrepreneurs? It's the idea that above all the challenges (that will surely come our way), above all the self-doubts (that we all have), there's a burning desire to make our mark, build something, and accomplish something of significance. Some of us just have an idea we can't shake. Some of us watch somebody else do something and say to ourselves, "I see how that could be done better." The entrepreneur in us may have had that itch since that childhood lemonade stand.

As I considered starting Swift Systems (my first tech company), I remember thinking, "Wait till they see me run!" Like a dog in a race, I could not wait to show "them" my speed, agility, and superiority. But when the starting bell rang and the gate was lifted, I was suddenly left with a vastly different feeling. The race was real and not at all what I had imagined. I had the idea that I would be great out there on the track, but it was not the reality I imagined. It was real reality.

I think anyone who starts a business will deal with at least some of the challenges I have faced. If you try to accomplish anything significant in life, you are going to struggle, and there will definitely be ups and downs. Here is the reality. You can have the best plans. You can invest appropriately. You can get the right team together. You can "do everything right." Yet, there are still no guarantees that everything will go the way you planned. In fact, you may even find yourself at "the edge."

When I was breaking this bad news to my mother-in-law, I didn't know if I would make it through. I was in a deep state of sadness and discouragement. The problems I had created were beyond the financial scope or reach of anyone who might be inclined to help me. I feared the worst. While I still got up every day and did my best, it sometimes felt as if I were trying to extinguish a volcano with a garden hose.

My best didn't feel good enough, and most days ended with the accounts showing a lack of progress and a deeper hole. I often wondered if I should give up and let disaster come because at least I wouldn't feel like this anymore.

Now, having survived catastrophe and having experienced a radical change in personal growth and wealth, I'm writing this book hoping to help other entrepreneurs. Many entrepreneurs don't realize that it's okay to talk to people to tell them they are going through hell and to ask for help. So, the first thing I want you to know is that you are not the first to find yourself in an untenable spot and you are not alone, no matter what you are going through.

### Survival, the father of success

I once heard the late Ravi Zacharias share that in India, there is a folk tale about a man on a tiger. Those observing the man were amazed at the man's bravery. Meanwhile, the man on the tiger was thinking: "Oh my, how did I end up here? Will I make it through the day, and will the tiger eat me?"

Never be embarrassed! If you begin to feel yourself and your company heading toward disaster, you should do what it took me far too long to do. I needed to 1) realize that I did not have all the answers, and 2) seek *wise* counsel and then actually listen to that counsel. If you stop reading this book right here, hang on to at least this one point: Seek *wise* counsel. You do not have to go it alone.

*John 8:32b: "And the truth will set you free."*

# INTERLUDE ONE

# THE NO-GOOD GUY'S
# JOURNEY TO MAKE GOOD

I'm a high school dropout who ran away from home at age fifteen. While it may sound unbelievable and not just a little Huck Finn-esque, I truly did climb out my bedroom window with a knapsack full of dirty clothes. I had less than fifty bucks to travel on, stolen from either my mother's pocketbook or my father's wallet. I don't remember from which parent I got the ill-gotten money because I frequented both handbag and wallet regularly with little regard for the fact that Mom and Dad had very little. That was the last thing on my mind, and off I went to travel the country and seek adventure.

I was a vagabond thief, a loser, and, generally, a no-good guy. However, I knew how to smile at little old ladies and make them think I was better than I was. After visiting most of the larger cities of the United States from Maine to Texas in two large circuits, leaving a trail of troubles behind me, I returned home. I had undoubtedly toughened up a bit and matured a bit as well, started a small business, and finally ended up getting my GED. Then I aimlessly attended a community college at night and later joined the Air Force.

With the Air Force's help, I zeroed in on a major in electrical engineering, but the truth is, I never finished my degree there either.

Since the age of ten, I have been working for myself in one form or another, and quite often out of necessity.

I grew up the son of a poor preacher, and if I wanted nice shoes like those of the other kids, for example, I was obliged to find a way to pay for them myself. While I figured that much was out of my control, I also learned hard work had its rewards, and the exchange of value was the path out of poverty. I failed to discover early on that even if I worked hard but did it poorly, it could also be the path to ruin.

### *"I couldn't figure out what I wanted to do with my life."*

In all fairness, I did have accomplishments, yet I couldn't figure out what I wanted to do with my life. I started out thinking I would pursue business law but lost interest quickly. I considered accounting but realized I preferred spending money more than tracking it. When I was in the Air Force, I received an excellent foundation in digital electronics and general electrical engineering. Still, I didn't feel inspired to stick with the military other than what was required to fulfill my initial enlistment contract.

At one point, I had what many might have considered a successful landscape company (at least for someone my age), serving the outskirts of Baltimore, Maryland. Here I was, only twenty-one years old, with seven or eight guys working for me. Our customers included banks, radio stations, builders, and lots of homeowners. I owned several trucks and equipment for which I had to rent space to house. However, I think I enjoyed buying and fixing equipment more than I enjoyed the work necessary to keep the business running. I kept trying to figure out how to run everything and direct people. While I grew in confidence regarding my ability to start and run a business, I didn't learn how great companies are built and run for sustainable growth and longevity.

My story involves several fatal mistakes, any of which could bring down an entrepreneur. They included confidence bordering on arrogance, a substantial lack of self-awareness in terms of my strengths versus my weaknesses, and a risky lack of contingency resources. As an even more introspective and astute Pogo might have said: "We have met the enemy, and it is I."

### The tipping point ... about to fail, about to fall

You're young and sitting at the dining room table, and your parents are reprimanding you for leaning back in your chair, warning that you are going to tip over. Of course, you don't listen. After all, you are just leaning back in the chair. What could go wrong? But then it does!

Suddenly, you go from being the kid who didn't listen to the kid calling out for help to the kid realizing it is too late. That's when you do not want to be held accountable for the risk you have taken. You just want to be left alone and separated from the consequences of your actions.

As adults, and for reasons we can't always explain, we take similar chances far beyond our control. We hit that tipping point. The fear we have as an adult is a lot like that of the kid falling backward in his or her chair, only the stakes are generally higher—much higher.

### New to the world of computers

It was early 1995. I was running that small landscape construction company I just told you about, and I was running it poorly. I was manually creating designs and proposals and tracking all our accounting records with graph paper and shoe boxes. It was a mess, and I knew it could be better.

Being new to the world of computers, I opened the classified ads hoping to find a used computer I could afford, but

I wound up buying something that was the technical equivalent of a boat anchor and just about as heavy. I brought it home, fired it up, and proceeded to install Windows 3.1, using the pirated discs a friend had loaned to me. I was such a newbie that I didn't even understand that I was pirating them. I didn't make it too far before I hit a dead end. The PC onto which I was trying to install Windows 3.1 was a 286 and had no math coprocessor. For the layman, that meant it wasn't fast enough or powerful enough to run Windows.

Before the bookstores closed that Friday night, I purchased a book titled *Upgrading and Repairing PCs*. At about 1,100 pages, it still resides on my bookshelf today, reminding me of what I had to overcome to enter and succeed in my current industry. Without taking a break, I read the book cover to cover. By the time I finished, even though I wasn't sure how to pronounce many of the technical words, I had a pretty high-level understanding of the computer's parts and how they worked, at which point I promptly fell asleep.

When I awoke, it was Sunday afternoon, and after some searching, I found an open computer store. After a few hours of overcoming communications issues with the proprietor, whose quite distant second language was English, I returned home with a few hundred dollars' worth of computer parts. I also had a renewed excitement to upgrade my computer so I could install the software and improve my business.

**It was beeping!**

I had been at this for twelve or thirteen hours and was beginning to think I had probably shorted something out and ruined all the hardware I had just acquired. To put this in context, I had just spent my rent money. As I considered how much I had overpaid for the computer I was trying to upgrade with all of these new parts I had just had to buy, I was on the verge of tears. It was getting close to 4:00 AM on Monday, and I felt as if I had made no progress at all.

With thoughts of giving up, a few actual tears of frustration, and a genuine heartfelt prayer, suddenly there was a beep, the sound of a spinning disk, and images popping up on the monitor. Dear God, I had done it! I had no idea how I had done it, but I had done it! I had gone from being someone who didn't even know how to use a mouse to someone who had upgraded his PC in one weekend.

The following week my wife-to-be taught me the basics of using Windows and answered questions I didn't understand when I installed the 3D design software that I had been so excited to use. For the next few weeks, I still ran my business. I still worked in the field with my team Monday through Saturday. I still wrote my estimates the old way, by hand. But I also took the time necessary to learn how to design projects the new way. Then I bought a copy of Peachtree accounting software and transferred several years' worth of financial records onto the computer. While I was fascinated by analyzing my business in this manner, I was also quite negatively overwhelmed with the data. I had hoped to utilize computer-aided design to crank out professional-looking proposals quickly, but I discovered that the technology was not much faster than drawing the proposals by hand. I could also hear the voice of one of my accounting professors, as I reviewed those first reports I was pulling out of Peachtree, saying: "Many new businesspeople fail to count their soft costs, their recurring costs, or their underlying costs of doing business, and it sinks them."

On the positive side, I overcame the pain of buying a beeping boat anchor and learning how to turn it into a working computer. Still, what I had hoped for—easier accounting and fast 3D design—had been replaced with a new set of painful revelations. I had a lot to learn about running a business, and my numbers showed it, plus I now wanted to be in the new and exciting IT field. My passion waned quickly for the business I had bought this computer to help me run. I spent more time learning how to use and upgrade the computer than I did working on my business. Instead of helping me improve the business, that beeping chunk of metal and silicon had inspired a newfound passion. A few years later, with numerous steps between, and I had started my first tech company, Swift Systems.

### Back to business

In 1998, along the way in my new IT journey, I was working for the E-services group. I excitedly offered to use my talents to build out a new service for the organization. The company owner was focused on what was of the highest value to his company (as he should have been), and while I was offering it on a silver platter, he said no.

Because I do not know how to give up and couldn't let the idea go, I ended up building the infrastructure for an Internet service provider and web hosting business anyway, but I did it in the basement of my home instead. Since I had sold my landscaping business at a loss, I worked several jobs to learn IT faster and pay off the losses. Money remained tight, especially with the needs of a small but growing family competing for resources with my never-ending hopes to get back into my own business.

As I contemplated a basement startup, one of the other major challenges was electric power. We lived in an area where power wasn't reliable. This meant the websites we were hosting would go down. I solved this challenge by installing a generator and wound up with another challenge. The reality of having an entrepreneur for a husband would hit my wife quite loudly when the power went out and that generator started up. Had I thought of making sure my wife could watch TV when the generator was running? No, of course not! And, to make matters worse, she was in the hot upstairs while the only air conditioner configured to run off the generator was the one in the basement to keep my expensive and yet unprofitable web-hosting servers and routers cool. As that generator blared loudly in the backyard generating electricity, my long-suffering wife would sit in the heat upstairs with the knowledge that the one thing I wasn't generating was money with my costly (and loud) hobby. Not yet, anyway.

However, during the next two years, my hobby-turned-business continued to grow. I began to sell ISDN-based Internet connections to local entities. Over time, I added T-1s about twelve times faster than ISDN connections (although today considered abysmally slow) and relatively expensive. I still don't fully understand why any organization that could afford such a cost bought the systems from me. After all, I provided their service from my basement, and some even knew it.

When I was ready to take the business full-time in January of 2001, I had spent a year working for an Internet startup selling and deploying an exciting e-commerce platform called InterWorld. When I joined the company as a new pre-sales engineer in training, the company had just gone public, was flush with cash, and was staffed with fresh new bright-eyed employees ready to expand the organization and conquer the world.

> **"It was an exciting time to be in e-commerce …**
> **until it wasn't!"**

Getting the offer from InterWorld was astounding. I had just been hired by a company that was quickly rising to spectacular heights. In a matter of years, the company went from a founder-funded startup to a valuation of more than a billion dollars, and then quickly it became worth about what you might pay for lunch. The DOTCOM bubble burst, and the good was getting thrown out with the bad.

The marketplace began to change quickly when investors became fearful of losing their substantial investments made in non-companies such as www.toothbrush.com. These were companies with little more than a business plan scribbled on the back of a napkin and two nerdy-looking kids with pimples who had just gotten $5 million checks from eager investment fund managers. When those companies began to fail, just as they should have, nervous investors couldn't tell the difference between a good company like ours with real enterprise customers and the small wannabes that were beginning to scare the daylights out of them. Traumatic as the marketplace was, the wonderful thing for me was that it was a year of rapid learning and incredibly significant income. It allowed me the opportunity to save up several hundred thousand dollars, which I used to launch Swift Systems formally.

**The first casualty ... the plan**

When Swift Systems became my full-time endeavor, I had a plan. I was confident that I could take my experience at InterWorld and do the same thing for other companies. "They" would be lined up to have me develop large-scale solutions—only "they" never showed up. The DOTCOM bubble scared everyone. It turned out that my target market of traditional business that I was sure would want to build large-scale eCommerce platforms were not interested in building large-scale anything until they could figure out what was worth investing in and what wasn't. So, having a fixation with food and shelter and realizing I was spending money quickly trying to run an Internet architectural consulting company in a down economy, I had to make some changes. Since it got even worse in September 2001, I asked the market the age-old question: "So what will you write me a check for?"

The new market need was this: Many businesspeople in my local marketplace had just gone through the exercise of looking down the shotgun barrel of "recession." They fired expensive employees first, especially those whose contributions they didn't understand, so IT types were vulnerable. However, it wasn't too long until those companies wondered if firing the IT guy had been such a good idea after all. That year was replete with massive computer viruses and other IT problems that quickly victimized those companies with no defenses.

**See a problem, solve a problem, make a living!**

It became clear to me that while my hopes for being an esteemed Internet architectural consultant had virtually evaporated, the opportunity to be a part-time IT resource for numerous local businesses was evolving. By the grace of God and the sudden absence of a market for what I had planned to do, the foundational skills of those "along the way" jobs (systems engineer, network engineer, and PC repair person) became the focus of Swift Systems: essential IT services for business.

Ten years later, people would speak about hiring a "managed services provider," but in late 2001, nobody had heard of such a thing. They also spoke about "outsourcing," but that often meant dealing with individuals in a foreign land doing their best to sound American while they assisted you over the phone. We could say that we offered "fractional services," but that led people to think that we wouldn't be available when they needed us. We did the best we could to come up with a term that fit what we were going to offer, and that was a "technology services partner." That meant we were going to figure out what to do as we went along, but ultimately, we knew it meant keeping their systems up and running and doing it cheaper—hopefully a lot cheaper—than the guy they had just let go. Over time, our services grew as budgets began to increase, fear began to subside, and our clients' need to stay ahead of their competition returned. We began to do project work and to implement cool new technologies, which was more in line with my earlier plan. But I was still just "getting by."

> ### While I rapidly gained IT skills,
> ### I did not progress as a businessperson.

The local IT market was growing as fast as the national market was growing, and we had few local competitors. My business grew primarily due to overall market growth, but the risks increased faster than the company.

In 2004, we added a data center operation. We eventually hosted government agencies that educated us on regulatory compliance and on managing audited processes. These things later helped us a great deal in the formation of HighGear, the software company I now run and will expand upon later. Swift Systems was now also hosting websites and web-based applications for many business customers, design firms, and other technology and web-hosting companies. We bought expensive upstream connections and began to sell business Internet connections over traditional copper infrastructure and eventually through a wireless infrastructure that we built over Frederick, Maryland. Despite the diminished focus this sprawl created, it was all working, and we were growing rapidly by every measure.

## The fatal errors

In 2006, despite a consistent five-year run of 50 percent top-line growth, I had made numerous fatal errors that left the business exposed. While I rapidly gained IT skills and progressed in my career at near light speed, I had not progressed as a businessperson during this time.

**Fatal Error #1: Concentration.** A salient example of my imbalance between technical and business skill was that we had two customers that comprised more than 60 percent of our revenue that year. No experienced, trained, or adequately advised businessperson would allow that. One of those customers announced out of the blue that in thirty days, they would no longer need our services. They had been rolled up into their parent organization, which would be bringing people in to replace us. Thank God, it took them a full nine months before they no longer needed our services. The other of these two key customers came in a few weeks after the first one and also informed us they no longer needed us. We never heard from them again.

**Fatal Error #2: Unnecessary Overhead.** To make a bad situation worse, we had just upgraded to a significantly larger office, hired additional staff, and made substantial infrastructure investments, which included a new data center operation.

**Fatal Error #3: Resource Depletion.** As a result of my overconfident expansion, our reserves were down to zero. We had bet them all on continued growth.

I had been unafraid to take these combined risks because we were growing at 50 percent a year and had enjoyed similar growth for the previous five years. I made the mistake of believing that the successes of the previous years would simply continue. We now needed more than 50 percent growth just to get back to zero. We were in a free fall without a parachute. I was also distracted that year as I attempted to raise money for my fledgling software company, and it did not go well.

**Fatal Error #4: Distraction.** We were in talks with a group of high-net-worth real estate brokers who were associates of someone who'd already invested in my new software company. They were all riding high on one of the strongest real estate markets in decades and were interested in diversifying their portfolios, and tech was hot. We anticipated their investment as a group in September of 2006, and I was busy preparing for that success instead of running my business.

**Fatal Error #5: Betting on the Margins.** Suddenly, our would-be investors' net worth was entangled within the rapidly changing real estate market of that period—the great recession was starting, and real estate led the way. For example, one of our lead investors had used "guaranteed sales" to beat out the competition for new listings for his brokerage. The downside was that when the market unexpectedly began to stagnate (six months before everyone else realized the market was crashing), many of his customers took him up on that guarantee. Instead of an abundance of cash, he owned a lot of homes around golf courses in southern Maryland, and their values were falling fast. I had made bets expecting others to come through without contemplating the vulnerability of their own upstream bets.

> *I learned the hard way that "Hopes placed in mortals die with them; all the promise of their power comes to nothing." Proverbs 11:7*

As the year wrapped up, sans investment, and with the effects of distraction and risk, my personal net worth and the combined worth of both companies was now negative. I no longer believed I was the super entrepreneur I previously thought I was. I was upside down and in big financial trouble, both in business and at home. It was getting to be a terrifying situation, and by August 17th, I received a letter from the bank that I'll never forget. I was already nervous because our banker had met with me just a few weeks before. He was visibly upset about my delay in giving him the financial information he had requested.

I guess I figured that if I delayed a few weeks, our story would improve.

I'd heard rumors about banks calling in loans, so the idea that I might be a target shouldn't have been surprising. Still, I was sure that if I opened the envelope slowly enough and prayed a little, the contents of the letter might say something like: "We need more information for your annual review." What the letter said was: "We have decided we want to 'exit the credit' and we want our money within 30 days, or we're coming for your house."

I spent that weekend in shock. I didn't tell my wife. The truth was I was never sure that she was excited about me starting a business in the first place. From my vantage point, her father had been a senior government employee, and when his life was cut short by cancer, her mother was able to avoid the financial catastrophe that can often come with that kind of a loss. Good federal benefits had afforded them a measure of safety. I felt, though I am not sure my wife ever thought or said anything like this, that I was up against the shadow of a good provider who had even provided for his family beyond the grave.

On the other hand, we now had four children and another on the way, and we talked about having more. Yet, my gracious wife who enabled and supported me heading into this undiscovered country, pursuing my entrepreneurial dream, was about to be led into disaster. Could I tell her we were on the verge of ruin? I had seen this catastrophe coming for quite a while. However, I hadn't been able to confront the reality of it until it was upon me. Telling her certainly wasn't going to be any more comfortable than coming to terms with it myself.

## I wish they had better shoes

I wondered what the lives of my children might have been like if their father had been smarter. I began to think about how my errors already diminished their lives and how it would soon be much worse. I wished they had better shoes. Growing up in poverty, one of my objectives was that my kids would never deal with the things I had to deal with as a child. I thought about how resentful I had been toward my father. I had judged him as an inadequate provider, but now I considered the possibility of my children facing more adversity and lack and facing circumstances that I had never confronted. This was the beginning of the mighty force that it took to humble the arrogant man I was and to help change me into the man I hoped to become.

Thinking back, I never really worried about signing that loan agreement. The fact that it had a problematic lien tied to our house was okay because "I was never going to miss a payment." I think I can remember telling my wife precisely that as I asked her to sign the papers with me. I knew I'd find a way to get things done. And, when everything started to unravel, we still hadn't missed a payment. But I had turned in rough financials the year before. While I may not have liked it, I knew the bank was justified in making their decision. I may be able to make the case that I could have gotten through with less pain and suffering if they had only been a bit more gracious, but I can't make the case at all that I deserved that grace. I didn't.

**But wait … it gets worse!**

The following week it got worse. This was another day I'll never forget. My head of finance called to tell me that there was somebody in our office from the IRS waiting to see me. He said her name was Miss Handle, and I thought he was joking. I glibly said something like: "Someone from the IRS is here to mishandle something?" I thought it was humorous until I realized that my finance officer, who usually appreciated my awkward humor, wasn't laughing. In fact, his breathing was unsteady. Then, as reality hit me, mine became unsteady as well. My pulse quickened. Minutes later, I was in the presence of a formidable and stoic IRS agent. I had the feeling that I was no longer at the tipping point, waving my arms about and hoping to recover; I was actually falling.

**Fatal Error #6: Not Paying Taxes on Time.** I learned that day that we were two quarters behind on our payroll taxes. We'd been illegally borrowing from the federal government to cover our operating expenses. Until that day, I honestly didn't understand the seriousness, nor did I realize how far into this ill-advised "lending program" we were. I had been one quarter behind in the past, but we were small enough that it never triggered what came next. I had always figured we'd just pay the interest and penalties.

Straight-faced, Ms. Handler informed me that I was now facing a public trust investigation and possible criminal charges; having the business shut down, the doors chained, our assets seized; and perhaps spending a year or two in prison. Now, the "fall" began in earnest. That feeling of weightlessness overtook me, and recovery started to seem impossible.

I started imagining myself in orange and wondered if my wife would leave me. Would my kids be too embarrassed to visit their formerly proud fool of a father in prison? I'm not sure I heard the rest of what Ms. Handler said. I only returned to reality a few moments later, fighting back tears and asking if there was anything I could do. Her deadpan answer was: "Pay the money, all of it, including the penalties and interest, before we complete the investigation." Now, broke and losing money by the day, I had a few weeks to come up with another ninety thousand dollars. I'd love to tell you what I was thinking, but I wasn't. I was just shutting down.

> *I was the kid leaning back in the chair*
> *who didn't understand what would happen*
> *when he hit the tipping point.*

There is a considerable amount of ego and confidence required when one leaps from entrepreneurial dream to saving the money, filing for the licenses, and putting up a sign. I was confident, perhaps overly confident, when I set out to establish Swift Systems, the business at the center of this story. Confidence is a beautiful raw material, but it is also dangerous and unstable, somewhat like nitroglycerin, which one can use to clear land quickly or open a mineshaft. Just don't drop it, or bad things will happen. My confidence led me to make some rookie decisions along the way. I was the kid leaning back in the chair who didn't understand what would happen when he hit the business equivalent of the tipping point.

Despite the seven years of pain and crisis that led to the lessons I share in this book, there is a brighter side. I learned these lessons and then began to apply them in late 2012. With God's help, between 2013 and 2018, we saw crisis become success. The "technology services partner" aspect had matured into the more straightforward "managed services provider," which fit what we had been doing for nearly a decade. We had to standardize tools and methodologies to meet the market's emerging categorical expectations. Still, those helped us accelerate sales and made us a better target for acquisition. The business name was flexible enough to cover the various services we offered. We promised that our customers' systems would run quickly, and when they didn't, we would promptly respond. What we did was still essentially the same. We helped people keep their systems up and running, and we did it better than the guy who did it before. By the way, we were still more cost-effective than hiring somebody internally, but that wasn't as important any longer. People had come to realize that technology was critical to their success, so what we primarily sold was a team of experts who would not let the customer down.

In 2018, after turning Swift Systems around from being a target for angry bankers and frightening IRS agents to having strong growth of 35 to 50 percent per year for numerous years, an eager buyer came along with an offer we couldn't refuse. That company was in the early stages of building a national managed services platform, and they saw Swift Systems as an excellent way to expand their presence into the D.C. Metro area. I bought out somewhat astounded investors, reinvested part of the proceeds into my next project, and paid cash for a farm.

**All's well that ends well!**

Today, I run a large and fast-growing software company built in the background during the most trying periods of this story. That company is HighGear. I'm going to briefly tell you about that company and my life today to paint a more hopeful picture of what's possible after disaster.

At HighGear, we have created a powerful, purpose-built workflow engine designed to empower everyday business users to rapidly design, build, and automate custom, enterprise-grade workflow applications for themselves within hours to days. HighGear enables people who can't write a line of code to discover, design, document, and deploy collaborative work and management solutions that can easily facilitate hundreds to thousands of team members contributing to complex, fast-moving, and geographically distributed work.

HighGear provides its customers with immense flexibility to continue to rapidly customize business processes on-demand, using only visual drag-and-drop tools to make changes in record time without coding, compiling, or rewriting underlying application logic.

IT workers are atypically open to this new model once they understand it because they remain in control of what they care about, such as access, authentication, and integrations with internal or external systems. HighGear's enterprise-grade security exceeds their expectations, providing the confidence needed for some of the world's most extensive financial services organizations to manage mission-critical work.

The point of all this is to tell you that I have emerged to run an exciting business with growth, rewards, and continued upward aspirations. Considering all the failures that this book exposes, it's a bit humbling to consider that some of the world's leading companies now depend on our product and team. It has been a journey from the edge of survival to the leading edge, and I hope that it also helps you dream and dream big as you consider that.

*Our failures do not define us; they refine us.*

It is my confident belief that while I can share what I have learned, it still may not be enough for all who read it. Why? It is not enough, because neither cleverness nor luck nor the invaluable assistance of other human beings can be fully credited for my survival. Specifically, I am confident that God (the Judeo-Christian one) has been gracious to me. Instead of what I deserved, based on my many errors, He has given me a life I don't deserve. This includes a kind, supportive, and beautiful wife and six kids who seem to like calling me "Dad." God has given me the exhilarating experience of building several businesses and more financial success than I could have imagined as a wayward youth.

# LESSON #2

# GOOD COUNSEL

It is not uncommon for leaders to tell people about their challenges. After all, the bigger the dragon we must slay, the more impressive we must be, right? What we really want from others is for them to say: "My gosh! I wouldn't know what to do with a challenge that difficult. Why, even Bill Gates or Jeff Bezos wouldn't have known how to solve that one!"

The reasons leaders become isolated are myriad, ranging from pride and embarrassment to just feeling defeated and hopeless. For example, the only thing worse than going through something difficult alone would be going through it with someone walking behind us, critiquing all of our mistakes. So we tiptoe into conversations where someone may genuinely have the answer, hoping he'll tell us if he sees our error, without telling anyone else and making us look bad. Of course, it would be unwise to share your challenge with someone you're not sure can help or who might be closely connected to someone who shouldn't know about your challenge.

However, just telling others what you see, feel, or are experiencing is not enough. Wise leaders, especially those up against new challenges or unfamiliar territory, will intentionally surround themselves with and *listen* to experienced, honest, and trustworthy counselors who are willing to speak their minds and offer sound counsel. When a crisis occurs, your view of the world is not reliable. You must be ready to take the "red pill."

## The red pill

The 1999 movie *The Matrix* depicts a digitized dream world created to keep people believing that they have everyday lives when their bodies are actually sources of biological energy to keep their slave master machines functioning.

Morpheus, a character who "frees minds," offers a pill to people trapped in the Matrix that disconnects them from this false reality, causing the Matrix to reject their physical bodies. This allows Morpheus and his crew of rescuers a window of opportunity to find and rescue them.

Morpheus describes the Matrix to Neo, a man he is trying to rescue. He tells Neo that the Matrix is everywhere, that it is essentially a false world created to blind people from the truth. Like the rest of humanity, Morpheus tells Neo that he has been living in bondage.

In the pivotal scene, Morpheus reveals a glimpse of the real world to Neo and offers him a choice between two pills. The blue pill would lull Neo back to sleep, ensuring that he continues with his life as before, blissfully unaware of his actual condition. Morpheus advises Neo that taking the red pill would cause Neo to escape the Matrix and experience real life, but that there is also no return. Neo chooses the red pill.

In this lesson, I'm going to advise you on where you can find your red pill. Be forewarned: There is no way back once you find out that you are part of your trouble or you need to change to succeed. However, I can promise that the truth really will set you free.

**Advice from the frog in a well**

There is no single solution for all challenges. And there are many faux solutions. Reaching out to your customers or vendors could increase your risks at a time that you are already struggling. Finding people off the street is simply not good enough either. So where do you go?

You may say, "I have a great team!" Your team members probably see what is happening, but do they care, and will they help? Or have you surrounded yourself with "yes" men and women? As valuable as the right team members are, they can't be your authoritative counsel. They may be the best source of information regarding the situation you find yourself in, but you need to remember that an inherent conflict of interest exists for them to tell you how bad things are or how bad you are.

You may say, "I've got a great group of friends!" If your friends are qualified in the areas in which you need help, this might work, but it's doubtful. It would be best if you remembered that your friends get together with you to enjoy your company. While sharing misery is allowed, it isn't going to be productive unless they have experience or wisdom to share with you about the business struggles you're facing.

Some friends will function as mentors from time to time, but what we often need to hear is what damages friendships. Good mentors, on the other hand, may not care if you think of them as friends. They want you to succeed because that is why they entered a relationship with you.

You may say, "I'll talk to my pastor about this." I'm actually a fan of that if you have a pastor who believes his job is to help you see the worst about yourself and that you may need radical change. However, few pastors have experience in wielding balance sheets, analyzing profit and loss statements, dealing with bankers, or the handling the complexities of running a large organization.

"The frog in the well" is a fable or idiom by Zhuāng Zǐ (and others). Sometimes it is also known as looking at the sky from down in a well. The frog can only see a small portion of the sky from her vantage point at the bottom of that well, and so her experience, knowledge, and opinion are somewhat limited when it comes to the bigger picture. My point is that your team sees only the agitated "We've got to get this project out of here by 5 PM" version of you. Your friends see only the wonderful you who's fun to hang out with on Friday nights. Your pastor sees only the penitent you who admits he needs to do better with his wife and children. These fractional views may offer some useful insights, but they are still only the views of the "frog in the well."

### "Good counsel" defined

Before defining "good counsel," let me first warn you of a particularly insidious form of bad counsel where you not only receive lousy advice but also pay for it upfront. There is a clear difference between the people who claim to have access to limitless solutions "if only you will begin paying my retainer" and a guide who has been where you want to go and is willing to walk through the difficulty with you.

As an entrepreneur who has already fallen for the spell of a shaman, I have learned the hard way that people rarely have magical answers. Solutions to life's challenges, especially business challenges, usually require relevant experience, the intellect sufficient to process complex and nuanced information, and the skill to translate all of that into productive results. People of the shaman variety often tell you they have packaged formulas, repackaged ancient methodologies, or exciting new breakthroughs based on the latest fad or a brand-new book. When they tell you they have an easy three-, five- or seven-step process that can be quickly applied to *ANY* organization or a "pay now and get results later" plan that somehow feels as if they'll make it worse before it gets better, trust your gut.

> **"People who have the experience to help you get through your challenge have been through the same or similar challenge."**

Then there are the guides. They are people who have the experience to help you get through your challenge because they have been through the same or similar challenges. Some are willing to volunteer. If you can find a qualified volunteer to offer free guidance, start there (especially if you are short on cash). Some free guides are merely doing it to reel you in, but who cares if you can test the waters before signing up. Then they can first prove their credibility to you by *showing* you that they can make some measurable improvement versus just *telling* you they can and asking for a fee. A guide would be unwise to engage a person unable or unwilling to pay, so a wise guide never will. But if you ARE willing to pay yet are currently unable to do so, ask for a bit of help to initiate the process, so long as you intend to be fair and compensate your guide once you can.

If you have multiple issues, you will probably need numerous guides. One guide or peer may be able to help you market your offering more effectively. But a guide's marketing brilliance does NOT necessarily mean he has any idea of how to help you attain better financing or to help you patent your product. Despite someone's impressive abilities in one or more areas, no human being is all-knowing. Everyone's experience is limited. People are not God. God Himself tells us to seek the counsel of many.

**The right guide for me was a group**

I remember driving by a formidable-looking gentleman walking toward the same golf course clubhouse where I was headed for a CEO roundtable meeting. He looked like someone who pulled up in a late-model German executive-class car. More than six feet tall with "executive hair," he was perfectly dressed and somehow oozed the air of success. I suspected I had probably already disqualified myself as his peer.

I was driving a slightly rusty and not well-maintained Dodge Durango with a noisy exhaust pipe that was spewing a substantial amount of unburned gas into the air. I had intended to hide my car out of sight at the far end of the parking lot. I planned to walk to the meeting in the suit I saved for days like this when I was posing as my alter-ego Super Businessman. I would arrive as an equal, with all evidence of my actual lack of success hidden away at the far end of that parking lot. Yet, somehow, I already knew that the gentleman with "executive hair" who saw me as I drove by was going to be my arbiter. He was one of the other CEOs in the group I was attending, and just seeing him there took all the wind out my impression-making sails. This was a harbinger of things to come.

**Equal parts arrogance and self-delusion**

The truth is, I had myself fooled. I was so used to faking success and making laughable excuses for where I lacked its evidence (usually explaining that it was right around the corner) that I had come to believe it myself. It was equal parts arrogance and self-delusion, because I had not yet accepted the fact it was I who had to change. At that moment, I believed it was everybody and everything else that needed to change.

Comparing myself to those in the group, I exhibited my arrogance and self-delusion handily. I was overcoming more obstacles than most of them, at least in my mind. I decided that since I ran a business that was larger than most of them, they had no advice of value to offer me. I discounted others who ran businesses larger than mine because they were not in the field of technology. I dismissed the visitors who attended the group with opinions that may or may not have been correct. I imagined that their businesses didn't have any employees or inherited money made it easier for them. Why was I so intent on discounting everyone? If I didn't dismiss them, I might have had to listen to them. As I got to know them (and myself) better, the feedback sounded eerily like this: "Have you ever considered that you might be part of the problem?" For months, I discounted these peers whom I would eventually hold in high esteem.

**Why I advocate so strongly for a peer group**

When you find a peer group of warriors with a commitment to privacy who are experienced, qualified, and trustworthy, and with whom you feel comfortable, this is the superior route to finding the solutions to your challenges. One person may know more than you or the others about taxes. Another may have a better perspective on sales. Another may see people issues to which you are blind. Our field of vision is about 120 degrees. (Actually, each eye has a little bigger range, but when the brain combines the images, it's 120 degrees. This is because we have binocular vision.) Therefore, we need others because their perspective makes us safer. With our futures and our fortunes on the line in business, why would we not want the additional vision from experienced peers? *"Without counsel plans fail, but with many advisers they succeed" (Proverbs 15:22).*

As an example, after navigating some very difficult situations with banks, I was able to offer extremely helpful advice to another business owner who encountered challenges in working with his bank. But I was going to receive far more than I had to give that day, as his deep experience in leading people helped me see something that was obvious to others but invisible to me. I had a key employee who had "quit but not yet left." What I mean by that is this: The only thing worse than someone you are counting on quitting and leaving is someone you are counting on quitting but not leaving. This is what occurs when his physical body is still punching in, but his heart is no longer in the job. A British marketing director I employed for a number of years, who was full of great sayings, called this "soldiering on." He described that as a state where you are still getting the "Yes, sirs," but the employee is just trying to keep his head down and not get shot until he can go home.

The problem I had shared was that I was trying to figure out how to hold someone accountable and get him to perform as I knew he was capable of, but I had failed to address the real issue at hand—his heart was no longer in the job. I typically would have spent six to eighteen months working on a situation like this, with things only getting worse, until either I eventually blew up and fired the person or he had it with me and quit in a fury. However, after sharing my frustrations with this peer group and receiving good counsel, I went back to the office, changed course, and confronted the situation head on. It wasn't a fun conversation, and it led me to facing some difficult truths (I was going to have to replace a key person). But by facing the bitter truth, we found peace and developed an exit plan that allowed us to remain friends to this day. He felt free, knowing he could now leave without crushing me (though I did shed a tear that night). I eventually found a strong replacement for him and moved on in with the business in better shape for the change. I had been working on the wrong problem all along, but I couldn't see it because the real problem was 100 percent outside my field of vision. I needed someone who could see over my shoulder and offer his insight.

As another example, our group reviewed a book together titled *The Blue Ocean Strategy*. The content of that book led me to see that I was marketing my business in ways that were not at all unique. I hadn't had time to read a book in years, but I was too embarrassed not to keep up with the group, so I bought the audio book version of it and listened to it on a long drive, and wow—it was groundbreaking! I had been fighting commoditization of our offerings on many fronts, and my response prior to this was to just "try harder," but that was not delivering any different results. This led me to take the group's advice and slow my sales and marketing teams down long enough to rethink the ways that we defined and sold our products. This made things worse for a while because the very team that I needed to "work harder" (as I saw it) was now huddled up in the conference room with me "not working at all"! But the truth is that we ended up "working smarter," and the result was that the business, which had been going sideways for years, was beginning to grow again.

We had made our offerings unique and more distinctive. This may be Business Development 101 to someone else, but I would not have taken this fundamental task on without the challenges that came from the people in my peer group. I thought the problem was that I had "bad salespeople." The real problem (that others could see so clearly) was that I wasn't doing my job, and those poor fools who had agreed to come work for me as salespeople had a "bad offering" to sell and a bad leader raging at them to bring in more leads and sales.

The root of so many of these issues that I overcame with the help of my business peer group was tied to my own arrogance. I believed that I could sell sloppy offerings, so why couldn't they!? I would never give up on anything or anyone (hah!), so how could this salesperson I have been demoralizing with my degrading speech ever consider giving up on me!? A group that came to see me as a valuable peer, but also a very flawed one, was also able to help me finally see what others had always been able to see yet I was unwilling to see. This happened because I came to trust the members of that peer group enough to accept their counsel, and that was the beginning of change and hope. I could not have done this by myself. I was literally blind in so many areas—as are we all. All it took was the perspective of others, and where I once was blind, now I could see!

## Alignment is crucial

I came to understand that guides don't necessarily have to be experts in your business model, field, or market. They do need to:

1. Understand the entrepreneurial spirit and personality.
2. Have experience as a leader.
3. Possess the same moral alignment as you.

Number 3 is a vitally critical point but often ignored or not even considered.

Joe Connelly is a friend of mine who owns a small chemical distribution company in Rockville, Maryland. Joe was not always my friend. When I first met him, I dismissed him as an unqualified advisor. I generally didn't like him because I thought he was a know-it-all who didn't listen to my brilliant input.

When I met Joe, I knew his business was a bit larger than mine, but he had been in business for thirty years. I felt he should have been further along, not to mention that he was not in the field of technology. I was convinced I had a fundraising problem. Joe had never had to raise funds. I was in a competitive and continuously changing technology business. Joe had been delivering the same chemicals for thirty years. I had severe staff challenges. Engineers were expensive and difficult to manage. Joe just had a small and loyal team helping him run his distribution business. By the second or third time I had met Joe at the roundtable of Christian CEOs, I had a long list of reasons why he would not be a qualified advisor for me, and that allowed me to stop listening to his critiques. Besides, I had started attending the group only because I thought I might meet some folks I could sell something to.

I have been a member of this peer group now for more than eight years. More than any other member of the group, Joe could see right through me. His thirty years in business and leadership may not have qualified him to solve all of his problems, but they certainly gave him the experience he needed to see quite a few of mine a lot more clearly than I was comfortable with. He has spoken difficult and challenging truths into my professional and personal life that I needed to hear, and more than that, as our relationship and trust grew, in a way that I *COULD* listen to. The truth is that Joe had a combination of attributes that made him quite uniquely qualified to be a guide, counselor, and advisor for me, but I wasn't humble enough initially to see that.

I was incredibly adept at seeing the splinter in the eye of anyone else, but I could not see the log in my own. For example, I continuously talked about how difficult my team was, but I was completely blind to how much I was dropping the ball on selecting, directing, motivating, organizing, and managing that team. I discovered that part of the reason why my team was challenging to work with was because they were frustrated (and rightly so) with having a terrible leader! It took somebody just as stubborn and difficult as I was to challenge me enough to see that I was part of the problem, or in some cases, most of the problem.

### They have to care about your best interests

You must find people who have undertaken similar endeavors, and you have to invest in them and not let it be about you all the time. It isn't easy to invest in someone else's life without developing an affinity for him. And if you do this from selfless motives, you are far more likely to develop the trust you need to know the advice he is giving you is rooted in genuine concern for your well-being.

Thank God, Joe and I persisted long enough to develop a relationship so that we cared about each other's best interests. What we had in common was incredibly significant. Joe had spent many nights awake worrying about keeping his team paid and his wife from suffering the consequences of his errors. He had hired difficult people who had abandoned him at desperate times. Bankers had turned him down when he had been doing his very best. Joe had dealt with extraordinary downturns in his business and had learned how to navigate them and recover. He learned to value my input (I think), even though I didn't run a business like his, and likewise, I realized that Joe didn't need to run a business like mine to be of value to me. The real value was that he was a fellow entrepreneur and a seasoned leader. Joe was a leader whose personal life would be totally diminished if he failed. That was more important and qualifying than whether we were in the same industry.

**Radical transparency and radical change**

Transparency is an intriguing concept. When was the last time we were personally excited about being transparent? Yet, until you can get an accurate diagnosis, you must be willing to share where it hurts.

It's challenging to be told, "You're the problem." If you want good counsel, it may come with feedback you won't want to hear. If you're not willing to be part of the problem, it is unlikely that you're ready to be part of the solution. I was convinced that I was not part of the problem until I had finally taken the "red pill."

> *If you want good counsel, it may come with feedback*
> *you won't want to hear.*

This is not a situation in which we should be trying to impress. I define transparency as the act of telling people (virtual strangers) where you are fearful, failing, blowing it, alienating people, or sharing your brilliant new plan that didn't work. I'm not saying you can't share good news in a peer group; I'm saying there isn't much use to it, except as a quick means to encourage everyone before moving on to the real work. A peer group should be a place where you can share what you are struggling with, an environment in which you can feel confident and safe because you are with people likely to help you and willing to share where they are having difficulties.

As soon as you're confident you have a trustworthy group, whether you think they are qualified in every way or not, it's time to take a risk. That risk is showing the group your authentic self, not the superhero you wish you were. If you build a relationship with a qualified peer group, they may just be the people who can help you make it safely through that dark room. You also now have an opportunity to encourage others to be transparent by way of your example so that they can benefit from the qualified perspective of others.

> *One of my favorite Proverbs is 12:15:*
> *The way of a fool seems right to him,*
> *but the wise man listens to advice.*

### Tears with peers, the beginning of hope

Let me spend a few paragraphs to share what it was like for me to hit rock bottom and to find myself ready to tell the truth, and how powerfully helpful it was for me to have that happen in the company of peers who I had also grown to trust and admire.

After a few months, reality came calling. My new peer group called me out, and I broke down. I spent more than an hour in tears, finally sharing the hard facts, including the high cost that this self-inflicted crisis was having on my marriage.

I had recently turned to my previously deprioritized wife, looking for comfort and companionship, as I had begun to accept the likelihood of failure. However, I had long trained my wife that I was physically, emotionally, and spiritually unavailable. Remember, I thought she should be thankful for the future I was working toward and told her so. She had finally decided that being upset about being treated as "a priority I would get to later after I had succeeded" was fruitless. She had figured out how to keep herself busy as an abandoned wife. Now, I wanted to press into the marriage as my grand dreams seemed impossible to achieve, but I had overdrawn the account. She had gotten so good at filling her time with meaningful things that she had little time left for me at all. She was busy raising our children (mainly on her own). She had become the super-mom of six children busy with performing household tasks, volunteering with homeschooling co-ops, and transporting our kids and everyone else's too. How could she possibly stop all of that now for a husband who had nearly forgotten her name? I shared all of this in tears with my peers because I honestly had no idea what to do.

I had missed so much time with my children and could feel it in the relationship I had with them. I finally confessed what I was confronting. I was trying to keep the company running because failing meant losing my home and succeeding seemed impossible. I had already been going sideways for five years at this point, and nothing was getting better. I desperately wanted a way out but had none. Again, this may not make any sense, but I came out of the meeting that day—for the first time in a long time—feeling quite a bit better. The men and women around that table told me that they had all felt the same way at some point.

> *I wasn't alone anymore, and that meant everything.*
> *I wasn't a failure. I was just another Edison*
> *still trying to get his light bulb to work.*

This honest confession was the beginning of hope. I had finally taken the red pill. I was sitting emotionally naked in front of a group of people I had initially tried to deceive into believing I was successful and wise. They had been kind enough to call me out only in areas where they saw I was receptive. But now, having provided useful advice for a few of them a time or two, and slowly revealing the real me and receiving good advice from them as well, I found myself in a room full of people I knew and trusted. I had been struggling on the verge of bankruptcy, worried that staff would leave, knowing that my wife *should* leave, and afraid that I would fail my children or already had. I wondered how I had let myself get trapped in this life where I owed so much and had so little. I couldn't think of anything to do but work while I watched everything slowly get worse.

### Discovering you are the problem

Even if I felt safe, it was no fun at all. Who wants to admit they are not in control? Who wants to make themselves vulnerable and face the fear of rejection at a low moment? If you're going to experience positive change, you have to be able to face the truth. While it wasn't fun to lay myself bare before a group of peers, I want to reinforce how much better I felt leaving the meeting that day. I've explained elsewhere in the book how my management style demoralized the very people whose help I most critically needed. It didn't change at all until I was asked, "Have you ever considered that you might be part of the problem?" Something about that day, something about being real, something about being vulnerable triggered something in this group around me.

> *By being transparent, I had triggered a form
> of love from this group so that rather than getting
> me to admit what I was doing was wrong, they were
> trying to get me to see what I was doing wrong so
> that they could help me get it right.*

I heard an excellent Bible teacher named Dennis McCallum describe the difference between "speaking the truth in love" and just "speaking the truth" as part of his exposition on the book of Ephesians. He put it so succinctly. He pointed out that the difference between speaking the truth and speaking the truth in love was that the objective of the latter was not to get someone to admit that he's done something wrong, but to get him to be willing to accept the help necessary to get it right.

You may loathe the idea of becoming this honest with a group of people you do not know initially, but if you take the time to build relationships with kindred spirits, you will understand why I am telling you that this is as critical to your success as water is to your survival in the desert.

If you are on the edge, don't try to go it alone. Find a support group composed of experienced and trustworthy peers who are willing to speak their minds and offer sound counsel … *and then listen to them.* Yes, listen to them. **Don't wait until you are in crisis!**

**Peer groups you could look into**

The group that I joined was a roundtable of Christian CEOs. There was an extra dynamic in this group because of a broader focus. We were trying to speak into each other's lives about how we could impact more than just our businesses. We were focused on how our personal development as leaders could empower us to use our companies to impact those we served and the world around us for Christ. That made a significant difference for me, but I would also humbly say that good counsel is not exclusive to Christian groups. Intentionality toward personal growth was more natural in the absence of competitiveness or "keeping up appearances," as I have experienced in some secular peer groups.

The following are a few groups I am aware of. In the Christian-oriented arena, there are CEO roundtables such as the CXP group started by my friend and mentor, Ken Gosnell. (Ken is also the author of an excellent book on business and leadership titled *Well Done.*) CXP groups that meet in various areas around the country are focused on examining leaders' performance and their businesses in terms of operational practices, current trends, general management practices, leadership techniques, and personal accountability. The CXP's "Case Stories" (where business leaders share issues and seek counsel from their peers) have been invaluable to me over the years, as have the one-on-one meetings with an experienced coach.

Another worthy group is C12, where I initially met Ken before he started CXP. The C12 program takes a leader through the equivalent of an MBA course in five to seven years while it provides a forum for twelve leaders to connect and share issues and concerns as they seek good counsel. This was incredibly valuable to me during my time in that group.

Another faith-focused group about which I have heard positive reports is the Compass Group, though I do not have any firsthand experience with them.

In the secular realm, there is The Alternative Board. I also know leaders who have spent years in the Vistage group. The feedback I have gotten on the Vistage group is that the material, leadership resources, training, and various large group events are excellent. Some have reported exceptional growth from both a business and personal perspective. However, I also know several CEOs who have reported feeling that they aged out of that program due to realizing their growth was limited by reduced transparency. They felt a need to show progress to their peers to remain respected within the group. Some of this may be related to the specific leader of any group. However, I have heard this feedback from two CEOs who were in two different groups. That is not a large enough data set for me to claim a conclusive opinion. It is merely an observation I thought worth sharing.

Finally, if there is no decent professionally managed peer group in your vicinity, why not start an informal one? Peer leaders may surprise you with their willingness to meet and engage. You'd be surprised how many leaders desperately need something like this.

# LESSON #3.

# PACK FOR THE ENTIRE TRIP

Unfounded optimism is a luxury that only the inexperienced will buy. However, those with the scars know that the first casualty in any battle is the plan. You'd be well-advised to have a plan B or C (and perhaps even D) as part of your plan A. At least be able to pivot quickly, because everything that can go wrong probably will.

If you assume your journey will go as planned, you are making a significant error. I cannot emphasize this enough. There is a high probability that not much will go as you plan in business, and you will need resources for executing inevitable detours. They are coming. The one thing of which you can be confident in today's world is uncertainty. Systemic uncertainty is a constant, a natural force behind myriad changes that occur continuously and quickly.

**Don't assume your journey will go as planned**

Jim Collins tells the story of Norwegian explorer Roald Amundsen in his book *Great by Choice*. The example is a good one for the entrepreneur. Amundsen was raising money to fund a trek to the North Pole. However, he suddenly switched to plan B. Americans Frederick Cook and Robert Peary had announced that they had reached that most northern point of the planet before Amundsen's journey even began. The sudden change in plans required Amundsen to race a British expedition under Robert Falcon

47

Scott to the South Pole. While the race to the South Pole remains one of the most criticized expeditions in modern times, it exemplifies that it is a good idea to have a plan B ready for when the unexpected arises.

## Resources necessary to deal with the unexpected

It is critical to have the resources necessary to deal with the unexpected. The unexpected *will* come in some form at some point. Perhaps as I experienced, it will be the customer you're positive will never leave you but then gets acquired, and the new owners don't need your company any longer. It may be due to the manager who always defended you but just resigned. It may be the contract you sorely needed to make payroll that just got canceled. Or it may be that aging furnace that just gave up the ghost in winter. If the unexpected hasn't happened to you yet, it will. So prepare for it.

Then there may be exciting opportunities that come along unexpectedly. You could have the opportunity to buy your competitor for pennies on the dollar. You could jump into a new market when a competitor announces he is getting out. You could hire that perfect person for your team, but it would take you a few months to get him up to speed and generating revenue. A new building that is perfect for your business may come to auction. There are dozens of these kinds of scenarios.

To take advantage of these kinds of opportunities or deal with any number of unexpected challenges that will come your way, you need to have liquid assets that you can get your hands on quickly. That means you need to forego the endless exercise of making everything better. I was a fan of making things better as you go, and I still am, but I had to learn to say "no" to my desires and my team's endless requests for more comfortable chairs, a better lobby for customers, newer laptops, and so on. You must resist until you can fulfill those requests out of an abundance of cash and not out of the first bit of extra money that appears on your balance sheet—and never on credit.

### Don't fear a downturn … fear going into one unprepared

As I'm writing this book, we are in the latter stages of the COVID-related lockdown of 2020. The marketplace is beginning to open back up, but we are also definitely in a time of unprecedented difficulty for many business owners. However, downturns are part of reality. They can produce opportunities, and those who are prepared can use downturns to win.

Downturns bring economic opportunities, and here is a statistic that may surprise you. Analysis of previous recessions has revealed that the rate of business failure is higher during economic recoveries than at the height of a recession. They fail at the beginning of upturns because the recovery requires fuel for acceleration, and they are out of it. If all you've done is survive, you may have nothing left while all of your new competitors come on excited about the bull market and hire up the best talent. You are still trying to pay off the debt you incurred getting through the downturn, and it can be a real challenge. The flip side is when you go into a downturn and you are prepared. Then, opportunity abounds.

### Great companies transform threats into opportunities

It is easy to say that challenging times limit success, but if you broaden your view a bit, you may find that challenging times bring opportunity. It is all about perspective. In an established forest, it is usually difficult for the small trees to get their share of the sunlight. But when storms, floods, or age take out taller trees, the open space left behind allows sunshine to filter down to the smaller trees below. Finally, these smaller trees and seedlings have a shot.

The Japanese have successfully mastered crisis management and view recessions and other negative situations as a mixture of both good and bad. They are aware of the danger and the opportunity, a perspective that encourages a focus on solutions to problems—not only survival but also growth and the long-term. A downturn offers you two choices: You can see it as a threat or as an opportunity.

Consider one of the many great businesses that have started during challenging times. Harley Davidson comes to mind since it emerged during the Great Depression of 1929 to the late 1930s. It reinvented itself amidst existential pressures from new Japanese competitors and depressed markets in the 1970s and re-emerged as an American icon in the 1980s, going public in 1989. Downturns may offer you your chance if you are ready. This is one of the many areas where fortune favors the prepared.

**Where and how to raise more funds for your endeavor**

First, the best time to raise money, whether through bankers, investors, or friends, is when you don't need it. That may sound counterintuitive, but it won't once you have been through the effort to raise money when you need it. Raise money during your up periods so that you won't have to when you desperately need it.

*Information you can bank on*

Banking serves a valuable purpose in the marketplace. Banks are a very cost-effective way to manage risk and to extend buying power. But bankers are not your business partners, and banks are not a viable contingency plan. Banks are spread margin lenders. They promise a specific percentage rate of interest to depositors (or these days to the Federal Reserve), and they will lend that same money to you for a higher interest rate. The difference between those two numbers is the spread margin. If they're lending you money at 5½ percent interest and paying half a percent interest, their spread is five points. They must pay all their costs of being a bank out of those five points. We may imagine the banks as institutions with lots of money, but only a small portion of the reserves typically belong to the bank or lending business. For the bank, those reserves are there to address the shortfall when a loan fails. If out of the 5 percent spread margin they are keeping only 3 percent after their costs, consider that it will take more than 30 loans that are performing to cover the cost of one that fails. With those odds, do you think they are in the mood for risks?

### Turn the tables on your bank

I would not recommend inviting a banker to your office and letting him hand you a loan application. Look at that application as a way of taking control. You are picking up a pen and beginning to justify that you are worth considering as a customer. You are putting your most personal information down on paper, asking the bank to weigh your worth. You are putting on sheepskin and entering the wolf pen.

Besides this, the first thing most bankers will do is go straight back to the bank and pull a copy of your credit report. Each time a bank pulls your credit report, your score drops. The more banks you talk to, the lower your probability of getting a loan.

Frankly, you are managing the psychology of the negotiation process all wrong.

The right way to find a banker is to turn the tables. I credit fellow tech CEO Nick Damoulakis for this insight shared in passing over a breakfast. I had run numerous Request for Proposal (RFP) efforts for many marketplace procurements, so how had I never thought of this for banking? Why not create a compelling document that tells the story of your business to go along with those bits of dehumanizing financial data and account numbers? Then turn the tables and build an application for your bankers to fill out for you. This works, and it turns the tables on who is being measured.

Once we produced a document that asked the questions and included the answers we were used to getting from bankers, making the case that we were an excellent prospect, we found that the banker arrived prepared to convince us that their bank would make an ideal banking partner. And more of them left thanking us for the meeting and asking about the next steps than we had ever received when we allowed the bankers to take charge. This turnabout of psychology sent bankers on their way excited about their great new prospect. Psychology has everything to do with banking, all other things being equal.

For an example of what you should include, please refer to *Appendix A—Preparing a Banking RFP.*

### About investors

There are several investor classes to consider: friends and family, angels, venture capitalists (VCs), and private equity. I'm not going to get into public markets, as that is neither the scope of my book nor an area where I have any expertise at this time.

### Friends and family

When I realized the money I had allocated to start the business was not going to be enough, I had to decide how to proceed. Here are the obvious options: Sell, give up, or find more money. In my case, I believed the business would do well enough to reward anyone who invested in it, and I believed it enough to ask friends and family to help me refill the war chest so that I could keep going.

Friends and family investors are just that. They are the people you know best who might be willing to invest in you. You should take on friends and family investors only if you have a clear plan to get them back out or show them significant upside within five to six years. In my case, it took closer to fifteen years, and those last ten were uncomfortable. That's how I learned how long the egg-timer runs on good will. So, if you have a legitimate plan that should reasonably take longer than that, make sure they understand when you think the return on investment will occur so that they are "eyes open" prepared for the duration of the investment. I failed at this by way of overconfidence, and it cost me. Going to family events when you are concerned you have failed your investors, who are also your family members, can be painful.

With that said, friends and family may be a great place to start when you require cash to launch, build, or grow your business. Just remember, if you wouldn't invest more of your own money into your endeavor, you shouldn't ask your friends and family either.

If you decide to have friends and family invest in your effort, hire an attorney. I don't care how comfortable you are with your friends and family; you need to do this. It will protect you, and it will protect them. It is the right thing to do. If you are in the beginning stages, any business attorney should be able to accomplish this, but I would recommend meeting with several before selecting one. This will help you to decide who you are comfortable with and to understand how different attorneys would advise handling your transaction. Do not take on any investors until you have incorporated your business and have obtained the services of a CPA, or at least buy an hour of a CPA's time to help you understand the tax ramifications (both ongoing and at the time of sale) and the options for structuring your company. Finally, you need to engage the counsel of a qualified business broker who has real-world experience selling small and medium-sized enterprises for their perspective on your end game now. You will thank me for this advice when it saves you hundreds of thousands or millions of dollars later when it is time to sell.

### Angel investors

I know of several businesspeople who have had success with angel investors. Angel investment groups vary widely. They are typically a group of high-net-worth individuals who enjoy meeting together and hearing the pitches made by entrepreneurs seeking to gain early-stage investments. Most of the success I have heard of with angel groups has been with investments smaller than $1 million, though I have also heard of some making much larger investments. Angel investment groups are typically less formal and often more flexible in terms of the types of investments they will make. They are most valuable when they also bring expertise that can help the growth of your business. Angel investors are least valuable when they think they are venture capitalists and want to measure you primarily on a financial basis.

### Institutional investors

While my software company probably will have closed on our first institutional investment by the time this book goes to print, I am still a student of this marketplace. I was first going to raise money in 2006. I explored various options, and the path I chose to take was a syndicated group of high-net-worth individuals. In a sense, we had created our own angel investor group, organizing it solely around our investment opportunity. As I described earlier, that endeavor failed because the group was populated entirely by real estate investors when the market crashed. Nonetheless, I learned a great deal about transaction types, structures, funding sources, considerations, and expected outcomes.

Institutional firms rarely invest their own money. Their money comes from the places you are already familiar with, but you may not have connected the dots. Have you ever noticed a "small cap equity fund" or something like that in your 401(k)? That means your retirement account is being invested in small cap (small capitalization) businesses. Do you think that your 401(k ) mutual fund manager is going to invest your funds into private companies and startups who pitch them directly? No. They are a fund of funds. What I mean by that is that you buy into their fund, and they buy into many other funds. Venture capital firms (VCs) and private equity groups offer up those funds. In turn, the institutional investors that you hope to pitch go and pitch your 401(k) fund managers, showing how they have gotten a positive return on investment in prior rounds. They ask for commitments so they can raise a fund and confidently invest in more small private companies, perhaps including yours.

The lines are often blurred between venture capital and private equity. What follows is a general summary intended to help you understand these markets as a whole and how you should reasonably interact with them.

### Venture capital

Venture capital firms, more commonly known as VCs, often comically (and mostly unfairly) referred to as vulture capitalists, are typically looking to make investments between $500,000 and $10,000,000. You can make yourself sound educated when you speak to a venture capitalist by asking such questions as "What are your criteria?" Their "criteria" will typically be something that narrows their focus by industry, revenue range, and growth. Another savvy question you can ask is, "What is your average check size?" It will make you sound informed.

Another essential fact to ascertain is whether your prospective investor is willing to be a minority investor or if he requires a controlling position. Some firms see themselves as buying the business while keeping the management team incentivized as owners to help them build the company into a wild success. Other firms prefer to bet on solid management teams and are perfectly comfortable being a minority investor.

Most venture-backed companies do not turn out to be big successes. For this reason, venture capitalists must fill a portion of their portfolio with companies that will turn out to be big successes, big enough to make up for the ones that don't go well. These savvy investors know that some companies will experience trauma. Venture capitalists are not in the business of helping you go through the kind of difficulty I went through. They have the resources to find success elsewhere. That means that if you invite them into your boat and it begins to sink, you are going to need to understand that they will not be interested in staying around and helping you bail. They will be pressing you to sell if you can or to shut down quickly and return funds if a buyer is not likely.

*Private equity*

Private equity firms are often venture capital firms that have a positive long-term track record, having transitioned toward transactions that will require more money and more extended periods to complete. However, the term "private equity" is also derived from the idea that there are private equity groups where the funds are genuinely "private." As I mentioned previously, the lines blur here, so realize that much of what I am about to say will also apply to venture capital firms. There are general partners, limited partners, and upstream institutional investors or funds of funds. General partners are active in the business. They might be the partners you will deal with when you pitch to a private equity firm. They are partners because they have funds in the firm, and they are general partners because they help manage the firm. Limited partners can be high-net-worth individuals, companies, or institutional investors who put money into a private equity fund but will have little management influence over the fund.

Some venture capital firms call themselves private equity groups, and some firms that act like private equity groups call themselves venture capital firms. How can you tell the difference? Sometimes you cannot. However, I have observed these typical differences. Venture capital firms are typically looking for a three- to five-year return on investment, faster if possible, and are generally interested in investing less than $10 million. Private equity firms are typically looking for a three- to twelve-year return on investment. They usually do not want to invest less than $5 million and may make investments that rise into the billions. Venture capital firms are looking to invest in companies with a clear growth pattern and offer a high probability of the forthcoming exit (sale of the shares). Private equity groups will often invest in precisely the same type of transactions. Still, they will also invest in strategic and sophisticated transactions where a business may not be growing at all but may be positioned over many years to be an acquisition target for a specific competitor or upstream industry.

The more "private" private equity firms are often "family offices," a term for a firm investing the wealth of one business and/or family.

Typically, but not universally, pitching to a private equity firm is not something you will do until you reach more than $5 million a year in sales. Still, suppose you are above that mark and can capture the attention of a private equity group. In that case, you may find it to be a more stable and long-term partner (particularly if the firm is primarily investing its own money and has a specific interest or expertise in your business sector).

*For key terms you need to know when dealing with institutional investors, please refer to Appendix B—Key Investment Terms.*

### Grant winners are not winners unless that is their business

While I have seen many research teams that have used grant money to make discoveries and build a product, I have never encountered a for-profit business that can make a viable long-term run out of grant dependency.

There are many economic development organizations run by municipalities and states and even federal agencies. For example, grant programs are available to help you get your first (or a better) website up and running. Grant programs also exist that can help you market your retail business if you're in a particular economic development area. You may also find grants to help you improve your office space if your business is in a targeted neighborhood.

I am not commenting on whether I think any of these are good or bad ideas. That is entirely dependent on your circumstance and what a program is trying to accomplish. However, if you build a business plan that is in any way dependent upon those grants, you are making a plan that cannot be sustained over the long haul. The organizations that award these grants are most excited about bringing new, hopeful, and promising entrepreneurs to the fore and putting them in front of a microphone to tell others how much the grant program helped them. Perhaps it did. But those same entities often tire of seeing the same individuals or business names come before them repeatedly. Grants may help get you moving, but they cannot be your plan to maintain your momentum.

Besides, the government is not your investor. Government agencies, similar to grant-issuing agencies (sometimes the same), love to tout their successes in helping businesspeople get started, moved to their community, overcome some specific adversity, deliver a market breakthrough, and so on. But the government should be a lender, advisor, partner, or investor of last resort. Government programs may be intended to give you a business advantage, keep you in business, or even to create your business; however, government leadership and priorities frequently change.

Suppose you build a business dependent upon the government (unless they are your customer) for preference, financing, subsidies, or markets. In that case, you will be doing yourself and your tax-paying neighbors a disservice. I have seen many talented entrepreneurs get sucked into this vortex and waste a lot of time and energy, reaching painful dead ends that come without warning when programs end, funding gets cut, or political moods change. The savviest of you will figure out how to leverage these programs for everything they are worth, but never as a long-term strategy for your viability.

*Five practical financial suggestions for starting a business*

1. **List all the things that you think you will need and estimate their costs.** Now double that, because you missed half of what you will need. Over time, unexpected expenses will arise in both your business and personal life.

2. **Double the figure in #1.** You will not regret having more set aside than you think you will need. You will quickly discover opportunities you did not foresee, and without additional resources, you will only be able to watch them go by.

3. **Set aside four to six times the amount in #2.** You're going to find that as an excited entrepreneur, you will be presented with all sorts of shiny options to make things better than you ever dreamed, and your business will be worth it.

4. **Now, imagine running your business, including the staff necessary to deliver excellence, for eighteen months without customers.** You are confident that your idea is so great that prospects will immediately overcome the fear of "but the business is brand-new; do you think it will make it?" and come running. Pack away enough resources for this challenging contingency, and if you succeed immediately, you will be in even better shape.

5. **Look critically at your personal situation.** Do you need car payments? Payments will reduce your flexibility in a crucial moment. Look around at what you own for the things you may not have time for in the future. Should you let their value deteriorate while you build your business, or should you sell them now to give you more resources? We all say we are committed to starting a business and will

do whatever it takes, but will you? Consider selling something that you care about. When you are desperate and afraid of losing your home, worried about missing a payment to the bank, or not paying your staff on time, believe me, you'll come back and look at that item then. Trust me, you will. I'd rather see you have the cash in the bank ahead of time than sell your treasures in desperation for half price. I have a friend who at the top of his game bought a specialty sports car for $65,000, only to sell it in crisis to a local dealer for $30,000 just nine months later. He did it to make a payroll and save the shame of driving home in a high-end sports car after telling his team he couldn't pay them. He did the right thing, but it would have been better if he'd had the $65,000 in the bank when he needed it.

# LESSON #3—PART II

# CRISIS CAPITAL

## Survival is a precursor to success

It is easy to get discouraged in the early years of running a business. It feels as if you're putting in endless hours laying the groundwork, and the list of things you need to do grows much faster than the business does. It seems that at every turn, there's another staple of business that everybody else has, but you don't yet. The point is that every time you put money in the bank, something seemingly urgent comes up for its use. I often began to feel disenchanted with the effort. After all, we dream of a market that needs what we offer. We imagine filling that need so successfully that we will be flooded with happy customers and going to the bank to deposit the proof of our now apparent genius.

However, the reality is that even if you have a great idea and people recognize it, many will stand back for a while to see if you survive. Before betting on your new and better service or product, they want to see if you will be around to support them. In the meantime, you will be spending dollars that you are probably not generating yet.

This is not a good time to be running out of cash. That is why one of the essential pieces of advice I can give you is that survival is a necessary precursor to success. You cannot get to the day where you are making impressive bank deposits until you've survived the days of making endless withdrawals, nervously checking your balance to ensure you don't overdraw the account.

I remember pulling up to a gas station to get lunch when I knew that my personal bank account balance was down to ten dollars. I needed gas to get home after work and back to the office the next morning, and I also needed lunch, having skipped breakfast. Imagine my discouragement to discover that my wife had beaten me to our paltry sum by thirty minutes.

There were many times like this as I built my businesses, despite having gone into it with seemingly significant reserves. I had saved up enough money to prepay all my personal bills for six months. I had prepaid the office rent for six months, and I had the funds needed to furnish our new office as well. I also had enough personal savings set aside to pay myself at least a fraction of what anyone else would have paid me for six months. I also had enough funds available to have a nice logo designed and to purchase the essentials necessary to go into business ... or so I thought.

### A banker's worst nightmare

Suppose you have ample reserves and want to keep a local banker on the sidelines for your unexpected contingencies and want to use the bank's money to cover your weekly payroll until customers get you paid. In that case, you are a banker's dream. If, on the other hand, the unexpected has come your way and you now desperately need cash to keep your business going, despite your excellent credit, you have become a banker's nightmare! If you already have a loan and have spent that as well as your own money, you have now become the banker's *worst* nightmare.

If you are in trouble with the bank, be forthright. The bank is not interested in taking your home. It is not interested in taking your car. And the bank is not interested in paying attorneys to ruin your life. It is interested in replenishing its reserves that you have put at risk and do so as quickly as possible.

Therefore, the best thing you can do is to communicate early and often when difficulties strike. Do not expect the bank to increase your credit line or to be understanding. Your goal in this situation is simply to keep them from making things worse. If you are heading into difficulty, do not waste your time seeking rescue from the bank. You will be wasting your time and theirs. You may also convince them that you are a fool for trying. Instead, and this is the point: when you do not believe you need a banker, a line of credit, or a working capital loan, **this** is when you should apply. Not tomorrow. Not next week. Now! So go back up and read Lesson #3, especially the section on turning the tables on your banker.

*Wartime profiteers*

Generally, venture capitalists are not interested in investing in a business in trouble because it could get better. They might be interested in a company that has already been run through bankruptcy, thus having new horizons in front of it. However, there are investors and investment groups that will invest in "troubled assets." It may be a lifeline for your business, but my point is that it will not be *your* business for long.

Troubled asset investors are kind of like the garbage collectors and recyclers of the investment world. Please do not misunderstand me; I do not mean to disparage them. They are typically sophisticated individuals who do the equivalent of what a good curio shop does, turning the forgotten and overlooked into value. However, they take significant risks on troubled assets and are not interested in how you feel about what happens next. I'm not going to spend a lot of time talking about this class of investor other than to say that if you have to go this route, it is most often the equivalent of giving up. It is unlikely that it would provide an exciting exit for you or other shareholders. You are going to get whatever someone will pay because you are selling something that may need repair or have limited value.

**Up against the financial wall, but not ready to give up?**

At one point, our business began growing, although we struggled to fund the growth and we were barely surviving. We felt that any reasonable banker should see that we were on the upturn, but we didn't know that the bankers knew better. They knew many businesses fail in an upturn, and any additional infusion of capital might only delay the inevitable. In the eyes of a spread margin lender, we were not a good bet. However, we confidently believed that we could continue our renaissance with additional resources, and we would not only recover but also press forward. I was confident enough that I was willing to guarantee the debt personally. I am not suggesting that this is either brave or wise. Instead, I am indicating that, with no other options, I was ready to do "whatever it took" to keep going.

Bankers were kind enough to explain to us what we should have already known. It involved ratios. A wealth of information is available online regarding the ratios that bankers care about. It would be a good investment of time for any entrepreneur to understand the concept. Your company's ratios must meet the bank's criteria. It is black and white.

Once you tell a banker you are losing money, or the bank's credit analyst figures out that your ratios are lower than its guidelines (which are usually very conservative), the banker may tell you: "We're sorry, but we can't help you at this point. We would certainly love to take a look at this again in the future." The naïve (and I count myself as formerly among them) hear this as hopeful. Maybe another good month or two, and then the bank will give us that loan. We will hunker down and try to get through. It is not about survival or progress. It is about the ratios.

If you are already up against the wall and find yourself in a situation where no reasonable banker will give you a loan or line of credit, despite the best dog and pony show in the world, there are still options. We found ourselves in a situation exactly like this, and by never giving up, we also found an alternative to traditional sources.

## Non-traditional lenders

Many business owners are not aware that there are secondary lending markets. I'm not talking about the guys who break legs if you miss a payment. Nor am I talking about fast turnaround online lenders who can simply get you to the answer "no" faster. I'm talking about non-traditional lenders that loan money to higher-risk clients. Of course, they will charge double the interest of a traditional bank, but they can afford a failure rate twice as high. If they make their bets wisely and only have the same failure rate as the banks (because they can see past the ratios), they stand to make a much higher return on their investment. Some accomplish this by focusing on a business sector the bankers don't understand. Secondary lenders are also spread margin lenders; however, they are just dealing with a more significant margin, which you will pay.

If you are in crisis and doubt your ability to get through it even with more resources, do not take their money. Don't take a traditional bank's money. Don't take Aunt Sally's money. Don't cash in your retirement account. The sick feeling in your gut is not to be ignored. Ignore it at your peril! However, if you are convinced you will survive by merely adding additional resources, then get over your *Wall Street Journal* rate-reading preconceptions and take a higher interest rate loan. A moderately high lease payment on some of your equipment or an above-market rate loan for your working capital is still likely to be far cheaper than letting it end up on your credit card, less expensive than paying late fees, and less costly than losing relationships with your existing vendors. And it is undoubtedly less costly than having to hire new staff because you failed to pay the ones you had while you were in the middle of a recovery.

Secondary lending is a real market. In our case, after being turned down by many banks, we began to look at the secondary market seriously. We certainly had to wade through a few time wasters, scammers, and aggregators who hoped that we were more creditworthy than we thought we were and that they could get a bonus for referring us to a regular bank. All of those were a waste of time. So, let me quickly explain how to identify a genuine secondary lender:

1. They advertise being able to swiftly underwrite a loan themselves.
2. They are not afraid of questions about where they get their money, and the answers may surprise you (e.g., your own 401(k), sovereign wealth funds from other countries, and sometimes the personal funds of the person who started the business that you are interacting with).
3. They will also be able to tell you their profile, which includes the types of companies they typically make loans to, the range of interest rates they usually offer, the dollars they typically loan, and the ratios they can tolerate.

I do not know if they will still be in business when you read this, and I have no current relationship with them, nor do I get any fees by referring them business. Still, the company we dealt with was Credibility Capital. I am merely trying to give you an example. Frankly, it was not only a decent and quick experience, but the loan ultimately helped us radically turn our business around. While we had paid off only half of the first loan, they extended us a second and larger one. The strength we had achieved in the business had corrected our ratios, and we were able to refinance the remaining debt with a traditional bank, cutting the interest rates in half and doubling our access to debt-based capital at the same time. Not every business will qualify for the secondary market. However, if bankers tell you no, you might do well to check out the secondary market before giving up if convinced you can use the capital efficiently.

**Five practical ways to discover "found money"**

Here are a few practical suggestions for the individual already in business and concerned about contingency resources:

1. **Review your staffing.** Some of your team members are contributing to your business and increasing your odds of survival. Some of them are staying on board halfheartedly to see if you can pull it off. Worse yet, some are enjoying the tacit agreement you have made to underpay them while they have covertly agreed to accept this agreement by under-performing in return. You should consider letting all of the last category go immediately. The folks in the "wait and see" category will be encouraged by your action. Now you can save the money you were paying the low performers and build up your

contingency resources. For the bravest of you, I'd suggest you consider letting the other category go as well and hire people who will not be watching and waiting to see if you can pull it off. When you hit your next challenge, have folks on board who will be happy to have a job where the mission is clearly stated as "help us survive." Most entrepreneurs believe there are no people like that. That is wrong. We all want to be needed. Hiring people and telling them you need them and their performance matters will inspire them to be the right people. This even bolder move will also allow you to: a) do what you can't imagine doing right now; and b) give your best people a significant raise to show them that you appreciate their hard work while you seek to hire peers who will finally contribute their fair share.

2. **Control your personal spending.** Many entrepreneurs reward themselves for surviving difficulty by making the day after any significant win a personal Christmas. "I deserve this," they tell themselves. "Nobody understands the risks and pressures I face!" Stop eating up your contingency resources with those expensive and unwarranted "parties" you have after short-term wins. We justify this self-destructive behavior by allowing ourselves to wade deep into self-pity regarding the difficulties we face in business. We are underpaid, underappreciated, overworked, stressed out, and tired. Sometimes, in the heat of battle, we lose sight of that long-term vision, and we begin to eat the very resources we need to win.

3. **Focus on your most profitable services and cancel the unprofitable ones.** I cannot tell you how many accountants or tax and audit firms I have seen that

advertise their services in the opposite direction of what produces a profit. I have met many of them at networking events and would ask, "What do you do?" The response often runs something like "Strategic business advisory services for Fortune 500 companies, sophisticated derivatives and wealth management, and tax and audit services." I do not mean to pick on this industry, but it happens so often that it has become a clear example of what we usually do as people, entrepreneurs, and business owners. We offer a product or service for which the marketplace will pay us, yet we talk about what we think will sound more impressive. We fail to apply resources to ensure that our core service offering is the best because we are distracted and focused on the service we hope will impress our friends. If you genuinely are a derivatives manager, fantastic, but what if you are an excellent tax and audit guy and you have now confused your marketplace? This isn't specific to tax and audit firms, of course, but by confusing the marketplace, you reduce your market, and thereby you reduce profits. I am suggesting a critical analysis of your gross profit's principal source, followed by recognizing that this is what you do. The time, money, and other resources you are devoting to being something you are not is part of the reason your contingent resources are not increasing.

*Focus is the enemy of failure.*

4. **Raise your prices!** One of the easiest ways to generate additional cash and ongoing business is to raise your prices. I remember having a conversation with two young doctors who had recently opened

a new practice in town. Both, speaking to me separately, shared their frustration with high student loan payments. Although they were as busy as could be in their practice, they felt that they were barely getting ahead of paying their administrative help and rent and bringing just enough home to keep up with servicing the school debt that had prepared them for this journey. I suggested to one that they consider raising their prices. I had to repeat that idea three times. The first time he laughed, and I'm pretty sure he didn't hear me at all. The second time he slowed down, considered what I was saying, and shared his objection: "We love our patients, and a lot of them might not be able to afford us if we raised our prices. Then we would have fewer patients." There is truth in his response. The third time I shared the suggestion, I asked him how underpriced he thought he was. He didn't believe he was underpriced at all. I had done some research and told him that he was 50 percent underpriced. I asked him how many patients he thought he would lose if he were to double his prices. With a panicked look on his face from the idea of doubling his fees, he said, "Probably a third of them." Yet it was simple math that got him thinking. If he lost one-third of his patients and doubled his price, he would immediately increase his income and work only two-thirds as hard as he was now.

Admittedly, there is something terrifying about raising our pricing. Still, we should be more terrified by delivering a good product or service to the marketplace when we are underpriced. When we are correctly priced, we can begin to build up the contingent resources necessary to survive the unexpected such as surviving a downturn. For the record, the young doctors raised their prices, and everything has gone on without a hitch. Fear is the enemy of focus.

5. **If your business is large enough, get a controller.** The human mind is fascinating. It can process vast amounts of information quickly and help us make critical moves. It can also ignore vast amounts of data when that information is painful. We are all capable of lying to ourselves. Set yourself up in a situation so that your spending is accountable to someone else who cares about your success. If your business is large enough, get a controller. A good one will save you more than they cost you, but only if you are also willing to allow them to control *your* spending. If your business is not large enough, you need a friend or a mentor who knows how to be unkind to you for kindness' sake.

## A final thought regarding capital

Once we had escaped the difficulties of being under-capitalized, I set aside enough money to get through the unexpected. Having learned a bitter lesson, I defended that war chest (as I called it) as if my life depended on it. When staff members asked for "this vital thing," if the only way we could get it was to tap into that strategic reserve, and even if they had made the case in a very compelling way, I told them we didn't have the money. If there was something I wanted at home and thought I could give myself a bonus, I told myself the money didn't exist for that either. That made it easier for us to get loans since we were able to show that we always carried a positive balance in a strategic account. Remember, a banker wants to make sure you won't fail. And someone who always keeps money in reserve is more likely to weather a financial storm. Resources will also increase your quick ratio, which is why you look more robust to bankers. Keeping an emergency account applies to personal finances as well, but I'll leave that topic to financial guru Dave Ramsey, whose books I highly recommend.

## The turnaround

This story would not be complete without sharing how I applied some of the elements of this lesson myself.

Not long after I had started the business, I went out and shopped for a line of credit. It was not easy to get one. Bankers have a habit of being fairly discouraging. They don't say such things as "We couldn't get this done, but I'll bet you would have a good chance with the other bank"; they say things more along the lines of "Your profit margin is too low and you don't have enough collateral, so your business is not bankable." And they typically say it with all the warmth one might find on the dark side of the moon. If you went in excited to tell them about your great business, and confident that you would surely get great terms, you're going to leave feeling a bit dissuaded when you hear something like that. What every entrepreneur needs to know is that banking is a numbers game. I had to talk to a lot of bankers to find the one who was overworked and under-staffed and didn't care about my details. She just wanted to close another loan and go home for the weekend. That may not have been an exciting way to qualify for my first line of credit, but I would not have made it through the first year without it. Therefore, I am very glad I did not give up when the first banker said "no" and told me how awful my business was and why no banker would ever want to do business with us.

However, as helpful as it was to have this line of credit nurse me through that first year, when we were losing more money than a blind sailor in a bad neighborhood, having it also blinded me to the fact that we were losing that much money. My first bookkeeper knew that she could withdraw from the line of credit to cover expenses, but I had never set up a protocol to make sure that she let me know every time she needed to do that. I was so busy bringing on new customers and excitedly growing the business that I had no idea the line of credit was exhausted until I came to her one day and told her I would need to pull about $20,000 out of it for a great idea I had. It was an uncomfortable conversation for her, but it was even more uncomfortable for me. I didn't realize we had used the line of credit or very much of it at all. I knew of about 5 percent that we had spent at one point, but now I realized we had no line of credit left. This meant there was no funding for my great idea. Moments later I realized it meant there was also no money for the payroll coming up in just a few business days. Gulp!

As you read through this book, you'll see that there were many ups and downs and that I wasn't a terrific manager of many resources, including banking resources. However, one of the behaviors I had developed early (of not giving up when someone said "no") ended up helping significantly when we began the effort to turn Swift Systems around from what had become a painful slow-motion failure to an exciting, revitalized, and growing business that would eventually get swooped up by a larger national competitor.

Later in that first year, we turned that dried-up line of credit into a term loan. That is something that most banks will work with you to do if you have kept your line of credit at the max for too long. You have made it obvious that you're not likely to use a line of credit correctly or get it paid back down to zero anytime soon. Once we had made some progress on that term loan, we had a business credit rating! We were able to use that springboard to go to another bank and get a larger line of credit. (Despite my enthusiasm at the time, this may not have been a good thing either.) Access to this resource allowed me to take risks that were "above my pay grade." Therefore, by the time difficulties hit, our debt level was significantly larger than the business could truly handle. On top of this, as I share elsewhere in the book, we also accumulated payroll tax debt, which is one of the worst forms of debt, second only perhaps to owing money to the mob.

As I shared at the start of the book, the accumulation of traditional debt (bank loans, lines of credit, credit cards, vendor accounts, etc.) and non-traditional debt (i.e., owing the IRS money—never do that!) all came crashing down just a year before the larger economy would crash as well. As the bankers and IRS agents realized that we were a hot smoking mess, they decided it was time to collect. We spent about five years making payments under alternative arrangements to both the bank and the IRS while we tried to keep the business open and thus also keep me out of jail. I will share in the next section how providence had a great deal to do with my escape from these horrible twin forces I had brought down on myself and those who were supporting me, but suffice it to say for the moment that it was no small thing to have survived. I was personally responsible for all of this debt, and my house and even my freedom were on the line. This is why I say survival is a precursor to success. Without survival, success is a non sequitur.

Nonetheless, I survived! And by the end of this period, much of the equipment in our data center and around the operation had begun to age. We had plans to get the business back on track, but we had no capital, and our credit was in bad shape. We needed to hire more people, but that would put more pressure on the little bit of working capital we had. So how did we get through? By many means, and here are just a few.

We moved to collecting partial payments upfront when we began work. We also started collecting more aggressively once work was completed. Combined, these helped increase our working capital, but not enough to fund growth. And most certainly not enough to both fund growth and the needed refreshing of so much aging infrastructure.

As we had not yet turned the business profitable, at least not consistently, there was no way we were going to get a traditional bank loan or line of credit. We were not exciting to investors, at least the non-predatory type, so it seemed that executing the turnaround we were planning was going to be impossible. That's where I began to take some of my own advice. We did not give up when the first banker told us "no." In fact, we probably filled out applications and tried to get loans or lines of credit with more than 100 banks. That is when we realized we were going to need to go to the alternative credit market. We had challenges in that market, too, but we began to find a few alternative lenders that could present options for us. We ended up working with Credibility Capital, the company I mentioned earlier in this chapter, and they were able to roll all of our remaining loans and debt into one consolidated instrument. This transaction freed up six figures of working capital, allowing us to finally refresh our core systems and equipment and to begin hiring again. It also reduced our monthly payments, thus increasing our cash flow.

No matter what happened over the next nine months, we made sure that the payment to that lender always went in on time. And to manage our expenses, we worked more aggressively than ever to reduce any unnecessary spending we could identify internally. For example, if an employee left, we tried to see if we could leave the chair open for a while and rebalance the work through others. If we could, we would offer the impacted staff a modest raise for their extra work so that we could save money while we worked to add more clients. Whenever possible, we also began to look for used or refurbished equipment to keep our infrastructure running. We would thoroughly test the equipment before putting it into production, occasionally requiring some repairs or upgrades to get things right, but even with the extra time invested, we were frequently able to save as much as 50 percent. Our combination of focus and efficiency allowed us to slowly restore our credit. With another year of "buckling down," we eventually showed a consistent but modest profit, and we refinanced our note with Credibility Capital again. This time we both improved our rate and increased the amount of free working capital we had after closing the new loan.

With another year or so of timely payments, our alternative lender had served as a bridge. We were now able to return to a normal bank and get much more competitive rates. I can still remember the joy we felt as a management team to be able to go back to the same bank that had called in our lines of credit and demanded immediate payment and see them reopen our lines at competitive market rates.

Within a year, we were able to refinance with another traditional bank, further improving our rates and setting up an even more generous line of credit. However, we had learned our lessons. We were now using our banking resources conservatively. No longer would I go to a bookkeeper or anyone else and suggest we use a line of credit for a "great new idea." That is not what lines of credit are for. A line of credit is an instrument used to handle an unexpected period of growth, an unexpected large project, or an emergency expense that is unavoidable. As our working capital increased, I decided to set aside the rainy-day fund I alluded to earlier. It may seem odd that I was using debt to fund savings, but I was determined that we should have an account with enough funds in it to either get us through an unexpected negative event or to allow us to leverage an unexpected positive opportunity. I wanted to be 100 percent in control of it as well. After all, I was responsible for getting us through the unexpected, and I needed to have my own stash as a last line of defense.

Keeping that money aside began to change our thinking. We eventually went from having that account populated with borrowed money to having it populated with money we had earned and saved. I had a friend who used to quote his father, who always said, "A penny saved is a penny earned." There is much truth to that. While we certainly needed to leverage the alternative lending market to get our growth engine reignited, it was ultimately our learning to live within our means that helped us to keep it going.

No longer would we spend money because we had a good idea. We were building and living by budgets. No longer was it going to be okay to lose a little bit of money this month because we were "working on something really cool" that will pay off later. We had developed a new discipline. We wanted and expected to be profitable every month. If we wanted to spend new money on something above and beyond what we had set up in our budget, we needed to earn and save it. We now needed to exceed our earnings expectations by more than the amount we wanted to spend. I won't claim that we always constrained ourselves in this way, but I will tell you that trying to constrain ourselves in this way changed our thinking, and that led to a very positive and visible change in our P&L and eventually our balance sheet.

By the time we sold the business, we had very nominal debt, substantial and consistent profits from period to period, and growing cash balances that allowed us to function as a healthy business.

Financial management alone did not achieve this. Good financial management is difficult to achieve in an unprofitable business, especially once you have run out of resources (regardless of whether they were earned or borrowed). We also had to invest in market understanding. We needed to understand what price point would allow us to win more deals. We needed to simplify our messaging so that our sales team could clearly communicate that to prospective buyers and bring home the orders. We had to learn to experiment with marketing, constantly looking for new lead sources and investing in scaling up the ones that we found could produce. We had to hire good salespeople, and we had to generously reward them for the desired behavior—bringing in high-quality clients.

When you feel that you don't have enough money to run your business, it may seem counterintuitive to generously incentivize your sales team. For instance, if you desperately need a new client, then giving the first month's revenue from that new client to your salesperson might seem crazy. However, motivated salespeople will bring you more sales. Unmotivated salespeople will bring you excuses. Would you rather pay a salesperson's base salary in exchange for their excuses, or a high commission rate in exchange for new customers? That may seem intuitive to some, but it wasn't intuitive to me, especially when money was tight. My peer group had to hold my nose in the rotten idea that I wasn't rewarding people well enough. When that changed, we had more customers coming in, and it got easier to manage our finances.

It's not just one thing that leads to a turnaround—it's many things. It's everything. It's self-discipline. It's good management. It's all the things your mother told you to do, and it's all the things you don't want to do. But when you make one hard decision after another, when you submit your practices, behaviors, and choices to outside counsel, best practices, and tough scrutiny, things have a way of getting better, but it's not an overnight thing. It's a journey, and it starts one choice at a time.

### Rescued by God

Even though I thought I had prepared adequately, I had not genuinely prepared enough to survive. I have benefited from learning these lessons the hard way. I should have "fallen off the edge" based on the decisions and errors I made. I can document many miracles that led me to genuinely believe that God rescued me for the sake of my family and so I could be of benefit to others. I cannot end this lesson without making it clear that my survival was not possible without faith in the providence of God to carry me through. In the end, I learned that God often rescues us not by extracting us from our challenges but by being willing to walk through them with us, if we will let Him.

# LESSON #4

# IT'S ABOUT THE TEAM

**You need people you can genuinely count on**

You don't become battle-hardened unless you've first been through a battle. Economic downturns, business crises, and problems with customers are crucibles. Countless stories are based on this very concept. A ragtag band of misfits comes together and accomplishes what previously seemed impossible because the team members have a common goal despite adversity.

> *You don't become battle-hardened unless you've first been through a battle*

During the economic downturn of 2007 and 2008, I considered taking on an investor to increase our survival odds. I figured I would find someone willing to take advantage of the situation and gain a portion of a good company by helping it through bad times. However, I quickly came to learn that funding survival was not an exciting proposition for most investors. The offers I received were either predatory or absurd.

Tony VanBrackle, whom I had come to hold in high regard for his business acumen and great success, considered investing but ultimately told me (as had others) that this just "didn't look like a good investment." However, he surprised me when he said, "Vaughn, how about if I just buy your business, help you shut it down, and you come to work with me?" It was tempting, for a moment, as he offered me a salary that was three to four times higher than I had been paying myself (and he knew it), and it was a way to extricate myself from a crisis.

I asked him why he would consider buying my business only to help me shut it down and offer me a job to help run his company when I was so clearly failing at running my own. What he told me crystallized my understanding of the value of people who have been through difficulty. "Vaughn, I can hire anyone I want to, but do you know how difficult it is to find someone who you can count on being there with you when the enemy starts shooting?" I came to learn that he was right. It isn't easy to find those people, and in my opinion, it's easier to build them.

The most critical element in the long-term success of a business is finding, positioning, developing, and retaining the right people for your team. While this chapter will be about the team inside your organization, that's not the entire team. Your team includes your vendors, customers, and advisors.

Choose your entire team carefully inside your organization and out.

### Balancing strengths and weaknesses

I was convinced that I worked like ten men, but nine of them were not paid. I suppose that is one reason I started my own company. Maybe you put in 10 or 20 percent more than the average person. Perhaps you have stayed up late at night to train yourself on something for work while your peers stayed up watching Netflix or playing video games. By whatever metric you measure yourself, you are willing to put in just a bit more.

### *A seemingly positive characteristic can become a liability*

I am willing to work endlessly. Many of the people around me knew that I would stay at the job late into the night and still be there when they returned the next morning. I just wanted to get the task completed rather than finish it at another time, even if it meant I had to make personal sacrifices and approach exhaustion. I was myopic when it came to the task at hand. I wanted to accomplish it with excellence, and I wanted it completed ... now!

Ironically, the people around me always seemed to be burning out. And I would leverage what I thought was one of my other strengths and give them yet another pep talk, which I eventually realized never solved the problem. My strength had become a liability. I gave myself a pass and convinced myself that the issue was "those people." Only, I was the one who had hired them. I was the one who managed them. I was the one who tried to motivate them. I was the common denominator.

### *"Aware of my strengths, but not aware of my weaknesses"*

I was not a good long-term motivator or manager, and I didn't see it because I was aware of my strengths but not my weaknesses. I had also never contemplated the idea that any strength one relies on in the extreme can become a weakness. To achieve great success, we must spend more time understanding our shortcomings and to surround ourselves with people who complement our strengths and possess different strengths that complement our weaknesses. This means we need to think less of ourselves, at least sufficiently enough to allow our team to be complementary. We, as leaders, are ultimately responsible for our team's results. However, if we fail to inspire others to become accountable for results in the areas where we are weak, then our team's results will be forever bound by our limitations. When you have individuals on your team who have abilities, skills, and experiences that complement your strengths as well as your weaknesses, you need to invest in them and coach them.

- Make them feel valued to bring out their best.
- Be delighted to see them and let them know that what they do is essential to you and the company.

This is when you can start to become a great leader, a great motivator, and a great giver. That is actually the secret, but you first must find people who are worth giving yourself to.

> *You first must find people who are worth giving yourself to!*

### The strength of others

Gathering the right people around you cannot solve this problem until you are first able to make an honest personal assessment. If you do not know or are unwilling to acknowledge your weaknesses, then how will you be able to tell when you have found the right people to surround you? Few of us can define our weaknesses effectively. We must build trusted relationships with people who will help us honestly inventory our strengths while equally honestly help us inventory our shortcomings. There are also great resources such as the helpful book and related assessment tools *Strength Finder*, which I would recommend as one of the practical tools (but by no means an endpoint) that can and should be used on this essential journey of self-discovery for leaders.

**The team with the best people wins!**

In the movie *300*, about the famous battle at Thermopylae, King Leonidas leads three hundred well-trained, battle-hardened warriors against a massive army of Persians. While the analogy breaks down in the tragedy of that elite force ending up dead, they do manage to hold off a superior military force through superior strategy, tactics, bravery, and commitment long enough to inspire their entire country into action.

At some point, you are going to face difficulties of various magnitudes in your business. Competitors will enter your market. Important customers will change their minds about you. The overall economy will surprise you just as you thought everything was going your way. Let's add this to the list of fatal flaws. Would you rather have people at your side who will fight to see you through or those exciting new hyper-qualified types who are standing by waiting to see whether you will succeed before deciding whether to hang on or flee?

**Selecting the right people takes due diligence**

I've got to give credit here to our COO, Josh Yeager, who encouraged us to listen to a series of podcasts on interviewing and hiring at a site called *Manager Tools*. The presenters were two seasoned professionals from large corporations. They had a wealth of experience in behavioral interviewing methodologies. The cost for accessing these materials is relatively modest, and I encourage you to investigate this online resource. The podcasts reveal how great teams are built. I had spent many years interviewing in sales mode, so the information from the podcasts was radical in comparison.

When I started out hiring people, I would talk the entire time during an interview telling the interviewee how excited

I was about the company and how awesome it would be to work for me. If the interviewee was smiling by the end of the interview, I hired him because I assumed he was as excited as I was, and that was exciting. But who knows if he had any idea what he was getting himself into. The other painful aspect is neither did I, since looking back, I should never have hired many of them. Of course, the hiring process improved over time, but we were still hiring far too many people who didn't fit our culture or who didn't possess the traits necessary to help us succeed.

### Due diligence in hiring

We had to abandon resume-oriented questions such as: "I see you were at Company X for two years. Tell me about that." Those kinds of questions created a platform upon which candidates could wax on in detail about their "wonderful" accomplishments, leaving out anything that might be important in helping us determine if they were the right fit for us. We needed to be using behavioral questions such as: "Here at Swift, we often have clients who call at five o'clock with a crisis, just as we are about to leave for the day. Our business requires that we do whatever it takes to ensure that the customer's business is not negatively impacted by their immediate challenge, whether we are about to close for the day or not. We have come to learn that we must do whatever it takes to meet their needs. So, can you tell me about a time in your past when you've confronted a situation like that? And how did you respond? Did it work out? If not, what did you learn? And please be specific."

We want to hear specifics, and we need to hear the candidate's stories. We want to hear the outcomes, and we keep digging to ensure that we are hearing real stories about real people and actual events. The person we are interviewing must be compatible with the behaviors we require for our business's success. Because the information is so readily available from *Manager Tools* directly, I'm not going to try to turn this lesson into a deep dive. Still, I feel the need to report that this was a specific weakness that became a strategic strength for us.

In all honesty, we have run the risk of exhausting candidates. In more recent years, individuals who have joined our team would readily tell you we made them interview with five, six, and sometimes seven people, often bringing them in repeatedly. Various roles require proof of skills through testing, all are required to submit writing samples, and some positions require a successful presentation as part of the process. If anyone already on our team has even a twinge that a candidate might not be a fit, no offer will be made. We have learned that quickly filling the chair is not helping us at all. It's better to delay a hire, even when we desperately need help, until we find just the right person who can become a permanent part of our team. While this effort has increased the cost of hiring, our turnover has decreased, and our team's effectiveness has grown in ways that all can see. These are the kinds of gains that are nearly impossible to replicate when there is high turnover.

### The Tennessee test

A friend of mine told me that he uses what he calls the "Tennessee test" when he hires people. If he is excited about the individual's skills, he would ask himself if he would enjoy traveling with that person from his company's Virginia location to its Tennessee location and back. If the thought of being alone in a car with the person for that long brings up negative emotions, he considers it a sign that the applicant wouldn't fit the company's culture.

Let me make this a command directive versus an instructional directive. It's crucial that you come up with your own "Tennessee test" and that you stick to it. Hire people who fit your corporate culture, and they will help you build your organization. Hire people who don't fit your culture, and they will do the opposite. I learned this lesson through trial and error and later rather than sooner. If you are starting a business, learn from my mistake and get this right. Figure out what you value. Figure out what your team values. And make sure they are aligned. If they are aligned, document them and propagate them. If they are not aligned, fix them. Your quality of life as an entrepreneur and leader is riding on it.

**Fire early, fire fast**

How many customers will have to tell you that "you can't send that person to *our* workplace anymore" before realizing that that person shouldn't be at *your* workplace either? It's not easy to let someone go, but sometimes it has to happen. You've got to decide to go forward with the best people, and that necessitates taking swift and courageous action when you know that someone doesn't fit. You can do worse things to an employee than disconnect him from a job he's no longer excited about or in which he's no longer succeeding.

One member of my team was so angry at me for firing him that when his wife came to pick up his personal effects, she took me to task as well. I remember being humiliated as she managed to get five to six nasty comments out before she got onto the elevator. They were personal and cutting, and the most troubling aspect of it all was that some of them were entirely true.

I had struggled for two weeks with the decision to let him go. I lost sleep for three or four nights. I had allowed his lousy behavior (because he was miserable in his mismatched job) to affect other employees' morale negatively. One was bordering on leaving if I did not address the situation. I'm not saying I was a perfect employer at the time since I certainly was not (and I still am not). Yet, because I finally had the guts to take action, the fellow I fired got a job that better suited him, and we found an employee who wanted the work we needed to accomplish and was excited to work with us.

### Make sure they will yell, "Look out!"

When building an organization, it is critical to ensure that people speak up. Once an effort fails, many people can tell you exactly when they saw it beginning to go downhill. It is easy to think that they are just exercising the benefit of hindsight, but the truth is most people do know when things are beginning to go awry and say *nothing*.

If you teach your people that what they see matters, they will share their concerns with you and give you their best ideas. They will alert you when an important customer is concerned about something (instead of thinking that you are too busy to bother right now).

I failed at this initially. As a result, my people knew that I would yell at them for disagreeing with me or diminish their ideas instead of listening to them. I would explain to them how their perspectives were wrong or otherwise reject their input, feedback, or critique. I did not realize I was doing it. I thought that I was just teaching them to understand my superior perspective. The truth was that I was training them that the 120 degrees that I could see was all that I was interested in. I was teaching them that I did not want them observing, thinking, or communicating.

I just wanted them to do what I had told them to do. The result was that I built an organization that failed as it scaled because when I was no longer on the front lines, we were virtually blind. The solution to this was to rebuild organizational trust slowly. I needed to convince them by my behavior that I wanted and would accept ideas, feedback, insights, and even criticism. Make sure your team members can tell you what they are thinking. Sometimes an environment like that is painful for a leader. Still, it will undoubtedly be more effective than the temporary comfort of being happily blind in the face of grave danger.

### Let them fail!

Great generals do not send their colonels into the field thinking that those colonels will never fail. They send them into the field knowing that they are committed and will do whatever it takes to get the best possible outcome, an outcome that will be as close as possible to the general's "command directive."

A command directive is one that states a result, such as "Take and hold that hill," whereas instructional directives focus on the steps, such as "Go to the bottom of that hill and then…." What if the best way to take the hill is to come at it from the eastern side and not the bottom? If you trust your people to achieve a result, you give them a high-level command directive. If you do not trust them or have not yet learned to lead in this manner, you will tend to lead through instructional directives, potentially stifling your subordinate leaders' creativity and growth. And you will be increasing your workload as you re-craft your instructions as each tactical circumstance arises.

To empower your team to complement your strengths and weaknesses (and those of their teammates), you must be willing to let them fail. Some people have strengths in different areas than you, and others share your strengths but lack your experience. If you want to empower them to grow, succeed, and reduce your workload, you will need to delegate. If the mission you have assigned to them is genuinely within an area of their strength, while they may fail, they will also:

1. Recover quickly.
2. Learn from their error.
3. Be willing to mitigate the impact.
4. Continue growing in other areas as well due to the experience.

Once you have found the person in whom your confidence is high, you must do your part and exercise the trust (regardless of the outcomes, at least in the short-term) to empower him with command directives versus instructional directives. Moving from instructional directives to command directives requires a high degree of trust. While this can be expensive if you hire the wrong person—and no amount of due diligence can prevent you from occasionally doing so—the benefits gained from empowering your great subordinate leaders in this way will far outweigh the costs. And if you have an organization full of subordinate leaders who are committed to getting you the results you desire when someone fails, the other team members will come alongside that person and either help him succeed or mitigate his failure.

### What is corporate culture? And if you lose your culture, you lose your company!

People will disagree on how we should accomplish things in business, politics, families, and society. Our ability to come to terms with those differences and then move forward positively will be based upon our relationships. And our relationships will be rooted in our culture.

After building two companies that shared the same office space for close to seventeen years, I have firsthand experience observing both the power and impact of culture. I would love to tell you that I was a visionary in this area, but that would be a lie. Instead, I was the unwitting student observing the flaws of my handiwork within one of those companies in stark contrast to the other. In that company, luck, favor, or perhaps Providence dealt me quite different results.

Team members at my first company generally expected bad news and difficulties. Team relationships were strained. People felt there were not enough resources and that they had to compete to get their problems addressed. People who made mistakes tried to cover them up. If friendships occurred in the office, they were primarily based on common complaints—not sports, not music, not politics, and not even what to do this weekend, but what stunk about working at my company. This is difficult to admit because it was all my fault, and I wasn't aware of it at the time. I failed to understand what was going on, even up to the sale of the company.

On the other hand, the team at my fledgling software company shared common values and connected easily. They had common interests. They laughed about similar things. And while they certainly didn't agree on everything, they were respectful of each other and enjoyed long conversations over lunch breaks on various topics. These strong relationships, based on shared values and common interests, translated into the ability to work through unrelated difficulties together with ease.

I remember taking a job at a company in my late teens where all of the staff loved football. I knew nothing about football. I once almost lost my "man card" at a Bible study when I tried to use football as an analogy and said, "Imagine you're on the 70-yard line…" Most of the males in the room erupted in laughter.

Thankfully, a few looked inquisitive because they also didn't know there was no such thing as a 70-yard line in football. Big guys making millions to run across a field and bump into each other just never excited me that much. Accordingly, it might not surprise you that I didn't fit in so well at that aforementioned company where football was the culture. If anyone who worked with me there picks up this book, they'll finally know why I looked uninterested in the break room. I didn't know what they were talking about. I did my best to fake it at times, but I didn't want to say something stupid as I had in that Bible study. I quit within a year despite liking a lot about the job. My point is simply this: Culture matters! Do we want to go through all the trouble of behavioral interviews, costly onboarding, months of training, and integrating an employee into our business, only to discover that he begins to burn out before we even finish getting him started because he doesn't fit? Of course not.

Our common interests combine to create a corporate culture. In this era of political correctness, the following information may or may not be received well. Still, I would confidently argue that it is crucial. Our corporate culture is not a reflection of us as leaders, although we play a role in creating it. Our corporate culture reflects ALL who work for the company and their values, interests, and behaviors.

If you have a core culture you like, you'd better define it so that you can own it, replicate it, and defend it as vigorously as I suggest you protect your profit. I have seen the corrosive power of a broken corporate culture and how it can impact an organization's success. I have also seen the remarkable power of a meaningful culture and how it can lead to a cohesive team that routinely overcomes extraordinary obstacles and achieves substantial and sustainable profits.

A culture needs to be about what makes your team and your company superior, and you need to raise the bar to where others can see it and then fight every day to keep it high. It will feel like a battle at times, but the dividends are well worth the effort.

### Values are not words on the wall

Your company's values are not just something you put on a piece of paper, your website, or a wall in your office. If you have correctly identified your values, putting them in any of those places is a terrific reminder to all that you must consistently continue living up to them to achieve your company's highest potential. But you can't just define some words and then pull people toward them. Instead, your values should already be written on your hearts and found on that wall for others to see. They are who you *already* are. If, as the leader, you value certain things that your team does not, you are already in trouble. You can write down your values and put them on the wall to remind you of what you want to protect. Still, if the people in your organization do not already inherently share those values, they will see them as corporate drivel designed to convince people outside of those walls that you are something you are not.

> *You can't just define some words and then pull people toward them. Instead, your values should already be written on your hearts and found on that wall for others to see. They are who you already are.*

### Values-based decision making

Here is a picture of the values we have on our wall at HighGear. These were developed based on behaviors around the outer right edge that come from their root causes or attributes that drive those behaviors. Ultimately, they flow from a center point that reminds us of our logo and brand. This defines who we are and the code of conduct to which we hold ourselves accountable.

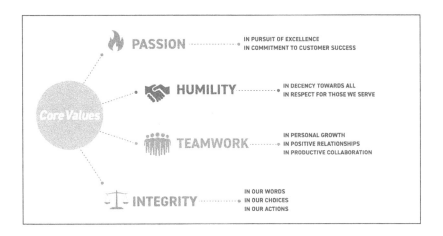

When you have determined your values and are assured they align with your entire team, you can now make core decisions based upon them, and you can do so more quickly. Consider our core values for a moment and imagine they were yours. You could now let a team member go because he has demonstrated that he lacks humility even if that individual is productive and otherwise amiable.

Suppose one of your core values is excellence, and someone displays extraordinary humility but never delivers excellence. In that case, you can weed your garden without fearing that it will affect morale. You can also decide whom to hire and whom not to hire. Values are non-negotiable, and they will help guide your major business decisions. Should we acquire that competitor? Should we submit this proposal?

Would it cause us to violate any of our values, or would it allow us to promote them further? Once this foundation is laid, you can use it to guide your decisions on investors, partners, staff, clients, and vendors.

Have you ever hired a vendor or gotten into a relationship with a business partner and just felt it wasn't working? The chances are you blew past a values-related stop sign. That is why you propagate and defend your values.

I cannot understate the importance of this topic. If you hire great people, motivate them to succeed, and empower them to lead, yet you fail to clearly impart your values then ascertain whether or not they will be aligned with them, you have made a serious error. Defining your values will help you be more successful, and you will look forward to going to work because you will have put together a family of people you enjoy being around and with whom you are succeeding. Still, difficult times will arise, and none of us want them. Tensions will flare when people disagree, but when you share a standard set of values, the probability of compromise is significantly improved.

### What binds teams together

The great news is that when you define your values and raise that standard high, people that share those values will be attracted. The color of their skin, the country they or their ancestors came from, their socioeconomic status, and the many other attributes by which we might be tempted to judge someone become largely irrelevant. Not that they are not important, but they are not important to fitting in. If they care about the values our team cares about and they have the requisite skills, of course, we have a match. Naturally cohesive teams foster a wonderful microcosm of organic diversity. People quickly fail to see the differences among themselves because they are drawn to the essential similarities, the aspects they have in common.

### *Naturally cohesive teams foster a wonderful microcosm of organic diversity*

"Community" can be broken into two words: common and unity. By having something in common, we organically achieve unity. People should trust that their most critical opinions are both heard and valued, even if everyone doesn't agree with them. They need to feel they are among friends, and they need to feel it based on inclusion, not words. Friends do not agree on every topic, but they remain friends. If you accomplish this dynamic within your organization, you will have achieved what most organizations struggle to do, and you will receive the benefits. I've experienced it firsthand.

# LESSON #5

# THE MYSTERY OF LEADERSHIP

## Not what I thought it was...

I started and ran a local contracting business. I was also a manager at a small sandwich shop in an upscale mall and a "student leader" in the Air Force during my electrical engineering and aerospace training. Despite this impressive (sarc) list of management experiences, I had never led or managed more than ten people and had never really been much more than a "boss." I had no formal training in leadership, no leadership mentors, and no real concept of what it meant to be a leader. I thought that leading just meant being smarter than everyone else, telling my subordinates what to do all the time, or maybe even just working more hours or producing more than the rest of the team as justification for being in charge.

However, I did have the good fortune to work for some great managers who made me feel appreciated when I arrived at work each day. One of those was Harry Sangmeister, who ran the shop that gave me my first technology job. Harry seemed to provide me with a new and favorable nickname every few weeks, always went out of his way to thank me for whatever little extra thing I had done, and congratulated me for all my successes. He also frequently told me he thought I would "make it big in this industry." While it was the worst paying job that I ever had relative to the current market, I felt terrible when I had to give Harry notice of my impending departure because the great opportunity I was headed to was due in part to the growth I had experienced working for Harry. I felt that I was leaving a friend or maybe even a father figure. As I look back, I realize what an influence Harry had, not only as a technical mentor, but also as a model leader who served his team members by thanking them, promoting them, and encouraging them. Harry taught me a lesson. Unfortunately, it was a lesson I wasn't aware of until I reflected on my interactions with him many years later. That lesson can be summed up as follows:

- The leader is not the one who knows what to say; the leader is the one who knows what to ask.
- The leader is not the one who says please; the leader is the one who says thank you.
- The leader is not the one who demands service; the leader is the one who serves and inspires others to do the same.

I don't mean to leave anyone else out who might deserve recognition for helping me become aware of what authentic leadership means.

Today, people who work with me often look at me in disbelief when I share stories of how I used to manage. I was so confident in my technical abilities that I was blind to my total lack of leadership. I was often given to loud and violent outbursts when things weren't going my way. I don't mean physical violence, but there were times when people would upset me so much that I would pound my fists on metal filing cabinets as part of a tirade meant to get the attention of the one who wasn't doing what I wanted. It often created what we came to call "the prairie dog effect."

I can remember slamming the door as I left the office of a staff member who agitated me and who had just gotten one long, loud harangue easily heard by my entire team. Other team members had been peering over the walls of their cubicles as they listened to what was going on. Then they dropped back into their chairs to face their computers as the door slammed shut. The prairie dog effect had happened yet again.

I was frustrated that people were letting me down, totally unaware that as the leader, I was routinely letting my staff down in far more significant ways. My lack of leadership skills meant that the team members were stuck at the levels in which they were hired. In other words, if I had hired a person who was capable of growth that could lead to increased performance and more significant contributions, it was unlikely that he would be motivated or empowered to grow due to my consistently lousy leadership. Consequently, not only was I at risk of demoralizing people and bringing out their worst, I was also failing to identify greatness and to figure out how to bring out their best. Occasionally, I would get a self-motivated person who would try to give me his best, despite my ineptitude. Unfortunately, I used it to find myself "not guilty" and failed to see that the common denominator among "all of those other *lackluster* employees" was me!

We had a high turnover. I was frustrated because people came and went. I complained, "Nobody is loyal to his employer anymore!" when the actual issue was my deficit as a leader. Frankly, it was ironic when I think about how I had hopped from job to job earlier in my life. I never asked team members about their aspirations. I didn't help them think through the solutions to problems. Instead, I tacitly encouraged them to bring all issues and decisions to me because I was more than pleased to show them how intelligent I was. I always knew what to do and say. But I was also getting exhausted, and when I was exhausted, I would alternate between helpful Vaughn and the guy known to cause the "prairie dog effect."

I needed to learn to help the appropriate members of my team become the subordinate leaders I needed. One of my customers, a wonderful, wise practicing Jew who had built a highly successful biotech company in Rockville, Maryland, sat me down one day and told me I should read a particular passage in the Old Testament. He told me that he knew that I oversaw sales, delivery, billing, and everything else, which was crazy, considering the number of people I had working for me. He mentioned Moses. Though he was considered "the most humble man alive," he thought that all Israel should stand in line waiting for him to judge their cases and resolve their disputes. At first, Moses enjoyed being able to solve the problems of all those Hebrews, but eventually, it was too much for him. Jethro, his father-in-law, suggested that Moses could appoint many capable men to solve lesser problems, and that only the more difficult ones would be sent to Moses. My Jewish friend called this the first recorded lesson in "Management 101."

### I never brought them donuts!

In the beginning, excited about having my own company, occupying my own office, and being in control of it all, I was exceptionally generous with the environment and the people. I liked to have a refrigerator stocked with soda and a big box full of all kinds of snacks. (Today, many pounds heavier due to snacking while working fourteen- to sixteen-hour days, I wish I had known what a bad idea that was.) I didn't have many employees then, so I would tell them to help themselves. They loved it! I had no idea how much they loved it until it began to get expensive, and I stopped sharing as the company grew.

Some of my early staff felt appreciated by that small gesture, which made me a great boss. Little did they know that I was selfishly thinking of myself, and I was only sharing with them because I didn't want to buy an additional refrigerator.

I didn't see myself as someone who should be delighted that I had people willing to come to work for me; I saw my employees as people who should be glad that they had someone like me who created jobs for them. This was an awful kind of arrogance. Instead of developing loyal employees who shared a common mission, that brand of leadership developed a loosely connected team of people who felt under-appreciated and uncommitted to the mission. Instead of giving people the opportunity to have a purpose, it reduced their workday to a series of tasks and clock-checking intervals. It turned what could have been an exciting mission for many into something far less—just a job.

In retrospect, my limited understanding of leadership and its responsibilities and potential robbed me blind. I had invested in building a business that hired numerous people and placed one of the worst leaders on my team in charge. Thank God I finally learned. Refer to my lesson on seeking good counsel, if you haven't already read it, to learn more about my journey from being a blind man to at least being able to see my errors in this area. I was able to see this leadership problem only by seeing it through the eyes of others.

As an entrepreneur, I had started the business with a staff of one: Me. I did every job until I was able to hire someone to do it. However, I wasn't good at handing off those responsibilities. When people would run into trouble, I felt that the highest value I could offer was to stop and solve their problem and explain what I was doing while I did it. I needed to understand that my role had changed.

Have you ever seen a coach pull out one of his players, grab the player's shirt, and put himself in the game? Wouldn't the coach's years of experience make that a winning move? As entrepreneurs, we may have a hard time recognizing that as our organizations grow, we are still responsible for the outcomes, but we are no longer in control of the details now assigned to our team members. Now that we have these employees, our job is to train, coach, and inspire them to function as a team that can react to the unexpected, deal with significant opposition, and overcome obstacles.

### Be a Chief Encouragement Officer

Lots of leaders aspire to the title of CEO. The best leaders realize they can be one at any stage of their career by choosing to be a self-appointed **Chief Encouragement Officer**.

Encouragement comes in many forms. It may include gently restoring someone who has failed, reminding someone of the progress he's already made, frequently saying thank you, noticing the accomplishments, and indicating that you believe someone is capable of more. It may also include concern for an employee's personal situation or advice when encountering an unforeseen obstacle.

Think of someone you worked for who made you feel valued. You couldn't imagine calling in sick. You knew you were essential to the operation of the organization, and you were needed. You felt important, even if other aspects of your life weren't going quite the way you wanted. You may not have realized it, but you were working for a true leader. The company was just a name, just a collection of products or services, but that feeling that made you want to go to work. *That* was leadership.

**Great leaders are great quitters!**

In many of the presentations that I have given on "lessons from the edge" before writing this book, I would have a PowerPoint slide with a single sticky note and the words "I Quit" written on it, followed by an exclamation point. Most of the entrepreneurs in the room would assume that I was about to talk about knowing when to give up or how to time an exit.

When my director of finance joined the company back in 2006, he was stunned because I set up his email and vacuumed around his desk. It's not that he didn't appreciate the effort; it's that he wondered if he had picked the right leader and if this was a sign that I would have my hand in every little thing in the business. He thought it would be challenging for him to own our finances as our first full-time hire with that title. The truth was that we were running so hard, nobody had time to get him set up, and his fears were warranted.

I was still involved in every little detail of the business. I reviewed every proposal. I checked our invoices before they went out. I conducted most of our sales meetings or at least designed the solutions we sold. I picked the color of paint in everyone's office. I recorded our outbound greeting on our voicemail. I even felt that I could order pizza better than anybody else in my company! At one point, I had thirty employees in my technology business, and yet I had written every article and document you could find on our website. For all that anyone outside the building could tell, it might as well have still been a company with one employee: Me!

The good news is that when people left, it had no impact at all. After all, I had already been doing their job. While hard work is a good thing, I had not yet broken the awful habit that many entrepreneurs have of doing a job while paying someone else who should be doing that work. This has a negative compounding effect. You are not helping your employee grow. You are doing what that person should be doing. That means your business will rarely move forward, and when it does, it will happen only because you decided to stay up late at night after everyone else went home. At the same time, you muttered under your breath and sent nasty emails out in the middle of the night because you were frustrated about doing all of the work that you never gave your employees the chance to do. And, yes, I did that repeatedly.

The reality is that if you do not allow your team members to help you, then things will go wrong anyway when you are finally sick, exhausted, or dead. Your legacy will not be a room full of people talking about how you helped them grow. And you will have died, as I almost did, doing all of the work you were paying other people to do because you didn't trust them, didn't promote them, didn't invest in them, and therefore didn't deserve to share in the rewards that a real leader gains from the people he or she leads.

> **Great quitters don't just quit doing the things they hate to do. They quit doing the things they love to do.**

Great quitters don't just quit doing the things they hate to do. They quit doing the things they love to do, and they empower the people around them to do those things instead. Because you love doing them, you will be able to inspire others, and if you encourage a group of people to be passionate about the things you love, you will multiply your effectiveness and will free yourself. You and your team of growing leaders can now continue to improve your company together as you deliver products and services to a market that is desperate to find people and vendors who are passionate about what they do.

### The unexpected power of vulnerability

What we have been taught about leadership in so many instances is wrong. As leaders we are already vulnerable to those we lead, like it or not. The plots of many great literary works center around leaders deceived into believing that their own people are their enemies. As entrepreneurs and hard-charging businesspeople (who might think of ourselves as less vulnerable), we are exceedingly vulnerable to these very same notions and fatal relational errors. Something as simple as the way we say something in a hurry can dispirit someone and set off a negative chain of events.

It would be easy for us to misconstrue our team member's response to our unintended offense. We could easily begin to see the person as hostile, allowing the situation to escalate into an employee who quits and leaves, or worse, an employee who quits but stays. Many books on leadership will tell you that you must show strength when you feel vulnerable. The counterintuitive thing to do—the one that is aligned with God's teaching and is the kind of common sense we often lose when we aspire to become leaders—is approaching the person with whom you are having difficulty humbly and exposing your vulnerability.

> *Matthew 23:12 ESV: Whoever exalts himself will be humbled, and whoever humbles himself will be exalted.*

Imagine an employee has gone home frustrated. He has complained to his family for weeks about what a disrespectful jerk you are. When he receives an email asking for a meeting, he will probably expect you to have a new complaint, a new demand, or a new hurtful critique to share. Imagine his surprise when you say, "Thank you for making some time for me. I'm not sure if I have done something to damage our relationship, but I have been feeling uncomfortable when we have interacted over the past weeks." Expect a stunned look.

"It's imperative to me that you are happy and productive, and if I have done something to injure our relationship, I can't imagine that I will have an easy time succeeding at my job if you can't enjoy yours. I felt that I needed to humble myself and ask you if there is any way we can improve the way things are going, or if perhaps I am just reading this whole thing incorrectly."

I once heard it said, "The more mature party is the one who looks for a peaceable resolution the soonest." As I evaluated myself against that statement, the verdict was clear: I was often the less mature party in almost every conflict I could replay in my mind.

A CEO who was sharing his favorite strategy for resolving conflicts said that he would start each of these talks with, "Our job is to build a bridge, and then get over it." I have incorporated that into my strategy. In other words, I want the people to know I am willing to spend enough time to assure that I have understood what I have done wrong and that we have agreed to new protocols that will make us feel safe and valued as we continue to work together.

### One team, one fight, but only one person rowing

The trouble with always being right is that you are usually wrong in some way, even if you are right in some other way. If people do not feel that they have been heard, valued, or appreciated, you can deliver the best motivational speech ever known to man, but when you turn around and face forward headed toward your goal—having just blurted out,

"One team, one fight"—you may find you are the only one who believes you are going in the right direction.

### *If you have not persuaded members of your team to their satisfaction, you have not persuaded them at all*

If you have not persuaded members of your team to their satisfaction, you have not persuaded them at all. You are not leading at all. A leader will make a case that the entire team wants to believe in, even if the leader must negotiate a slightly different course. Then, instead of only one person rowing, *everyone* will be rowing.

This kind of leadership requires relationship, and relationship requires give and take. That means that as the leader, you're going to have to relinquish things that may feel very important to you from time to time. By doing so, you can inspire your team to offer up the same flexibility when you need it back. This kind of relationship cannot be developed without the counterintuitive things I have described above. You cannot get to know someone deeply without revealing yourself deeply. You cannot lead someone effectively without exposing the significant concerns that all leaders share, that we are not doing our job effectively in one or more areas. The intuitive thing to do is to hire people who can make up for our weaknesses. The counterintuitive thing to do is to expose our weaknesses and ask people to help.

### Pride cometh before a fall

I had prepared a comprehensive presentation. I filled it with compelling examples and authoritative quotes. I used these to wrap a series of new initiatives that I was sure would breathe life into this unexcited group of church volunteers. I had thought of everything, including snacks, chair arrangements, projector, extension cord, projection screen, and so on. The only thing that was missing was one single person who cared one bit about my self-proclaimed brilliant ideas. Trying to lead a group of tired and discouraged volunteers taught me an important lesson.

The root of my error was that I wasn't there to serve them at all, which meant I really wasn't there to lead them either. I thought that I was awesome and that they should follow me. John Maxwell (whose book on the five levels of leadership I highly recommend) says that if you set out on a mission and realize that no one is following you, you are not leading a mission—you are just going on a walk. I was not only just going on a walk in this situation; I was also frustrating and offending the very people I had assumed I would energize and transform.

I returned to my day job as a business owner and leader with a new and painful realization. I was leading my companies the same way I had tried to lead that group of church volunteers. Thank God, I began to see that I was part of the problem. It took several years (and it is still an ongoing journey) for me to learn that if I wanted to truly lead, I needed to understand the hopes, dreams, aspirations, frustrations, needs, and goals of the people I was leading. Money can buy you employees, but it cannot buy you a team. And being in charge doesn't make you a leader.

If you see your job as a leader as understanding and inspiring your people to do *their* most outstanding work and helping them achieve their greatness, you will be headed in the right direction. If you think of yourself as responsible for finding opportunities that allow your people to rise on the way to what they are capable of, you will be headed in the right direction. If you think of yourself as creating a team that will eventually not need you at all, you will also be headed in the right direction. Lao Tzu expresses this concept well: "A leader is best when people barely know he exists. When his work is done, his aim fulfilled, they will say, 'We did it ourselves.'"

# LESSON #6

# LEARNING HOW TO SELL

They say there are two kinds of people who start a business: the ones who have a big idea and hope they can sell it, and the ones who can sell anything and have found something to sell. I was one of the former types, believing I could deliver a better product or service. If unlike me, you are one of those people who have started or are considering starting your business after ten years of professional sales and marketing experience, you may want to skip this chapter. But if you started your business because you are passionate about your product or service and are now facing challenges associated with sales, I hope that I can assist you by sharing what I learned along the way.

### Getting to the bottom line

Have you ever gone shopping and run into an "experienced salesperson," one who was more interested in "building a rapport" or "assessing your needs" or "building a value proposition" than in just answering your questions and selling you something you already knew you needed? Your prospects need to be able to quickly understand and evaluate what you are selling.

Some say that selling is all about a relationship. Some will tell you it's all about the solution. Some will say it's about correctly assessing your prospect's needs, while others will tell you it's about having the best price. Then, if you are a realtor, there is "location, location, location!" Maybe in the current world, that means a great domain name or a well-placed digital ad, but here's the reality, and it's not new: people don't want to buy what you want to sell … ever. They have problems, needs, or desires, and what they are interested in is having their needs, wants, or desires satisfied. They don't want a complicated process.

Potential customers don't want your thorough analysis (unless they do!). They don't want to spend their time answering seemingly endless questions. This is not to suggest that some sales efforts will not warrant a sophisticated process. However, our world is increasingly busy, and most people want to get to the bottom line as quickly as possible.

### Know what your prospects and customers look like

Initially, our target market was anybody who would write a check. When you are starting, that may be all right, although it probably isn't. But once you have been in business for a while, you'd better refine your pitch. You'd better know who you are and what you are selling, and it must come across clearly enough to engage someone who requires what you are selling.

For my current company, HighGear, we have learned what a prospect looks like and what their current problem looks like, and what kind of human resources they will need on their team to be successful with our software. We have learned that we are most compelling to departmental leaders who manage at least 25 people, or multi-departmental directors in companies with 150 to 150,000 employees who have a clear first work-related need, a process-ready organization, an executive sponsor, and a subject matter expert or business analyst on their team(s) who would be excited to learn how we empower non-programmers to do what used to require programmers. We have defined who we want to sell to, and that makes it easier to identify our prospects.

**Package it!**

Would you like to sell more of what you are bringing to the market? Would you like to get more for your product than your competitors do? Then stop and think like the person on the other side of that transaction for a moment. What do we need to do to make it easy for your prospect to find, justify, and buy your product?

We are entrepreneurs! We are good at making up everything on the fly. People used to ask me, "What does your company do?" I'd tell them that we have all sorts of fantastic services and that we do a little bit of this and a little bit of that. I would make it all up as I went along, based on what I thought they needed. I would go on and on, looking for a sign that something was resonating with the prospect, and then either drill in or talk faster to make sure I got everything in. Eventually, the prospect would tell me to stop and would often add that he had no idea what my company did, let alone ask how to purchase anything.

"What on earth does your company do?"

We had to refine our pitch so that we could tell our prospects, "We do A, B, and C, and here are the packages or tiers we offer." While entrepreneurs often fear limiting their product or service this way, there is always customization. However, we can't sell something a buyer can't comprehend, and packaging facilitates that. It also helps us build a sales team. When customization is introduced, we are now negotiating specific, prospect-selected deliverables. Without a package, we would not have that starting point.

While running my contracting business in my college days, I would run out of work in winter and would begin selling firewood. In my best year, I sold 1,200 cords in the

Baltimore metropolitan area. (To give you an idea of how much wood that is, the bed of a full-sized pickup truck tightly packed full of split firewood would be about half a cord.) I discovered that many of my competitors failed to offer a critically important service. That service was stacking, i.e., taking the wood around to someone's back-yard and putting it in the rack instead of leaving it in the customer's driveway in a pile.

We became the only company that would carry the wood to wherever a customer wanted it, and we would stack it for him as well. The fees varied dramatically. They had to. But when we said that stacking was available and we would negotiate the fee upon arrival, no one wanted to order fire-wood from us. When we said that stacking was $35, which sounded like a reasonable price, and we also disclosed that there might be an extra charge if stairs or gates were involved, most folks were convinced the cost would be $35 for them because they were charming and they would tip the delivery people. We generally charged $35 unless it was something truly atypical, but even then, we had beaten the competi-tion since we already had the order for the firewood. All we had to do now was negotiate a fair fee so that the customer would be happy and keep calling us back. I had created a second business by merely packaging two essential services together, making the purchase easy. Most of my competi-tors, if I would run into them, were aware of who we were. We were an enigma to them. And the competition couldn't understand how a twenty-year-old kid was getting $20 a cord more for firewood than they were. The answer was simple: they were selling firewood; I was selling a package.

Sometimes it is as simple as figuring out what a market wants and bundling products and services to make the buying decision simpler while increasing the perceived value of the items within the offering.

**Example A.** Does nine dollars seem like a lot for a sandwich? How about a meal that lets one pick a soup, a sandwich, a small side, and a drink? The focus switches from the price of each item to deciding which sandwich to choose. In your business, you could probably use the same concept.

**Example B.** If you sell automotive services, you may think that your business is too complicated for something like this. But have you ever considered how difficult it is to recruit and retain mechanics and how easy it might be to recruit and retain drivers? What if any customer could call you and have a car picked up and a loaner left in its place, no matter the location? An innovative automotive repair business might buy an inexpensive rental car franchise and offer pickup of the customer's car and delivery of a loaner car for a fee of $100 every time one needed service. Of course, you're going to charge more for the repairs. But at least the car is already at your shop. If you have a long line of cars to repair, it will be easier to recruit and retain mechanics. If you have more than enough customers to steadily fund your business, it will make it exciting for mechanics to work for you.

**Example C.** I believe the medical industry is also ripe for packaging. Imagine a doctor who charges you a small monthly retainer for regular and preferential access (adjusted from time to time based on age and need), allowing for phone calls within a reasonable time frame instead of having to make an appointment and going to the doctor's office. This would not be telemedicine, and it would be geared to busy folks. The doctor would produce a steady stream of income from another profit center by offering something innovative, a simple-to-order package plan of up to four calls a month, up to two emergency calls per year, and a response time within four hours for non-emergencies. The IT industry was initially resistant to this concept of "managed services." Still, it has proven to be an excellent business model that is far more predictable in terms of supply, demand, capacity, income, and other essential metrics than anyone would've expected.

The last two examples I've given have exemplified either packaging something in a way that is different from what the market is used to or packaging two things together that the market is used to receiving individually, but not in combination.

**Example D.** Many accountants charge their customers by the hour for most of what they do throughout the year and have packaging only around standardized services such as payroll and annual tax returns. But what if you called a small business accountant who said for a company your size, we would typically charge $1,000 a month, and you could contact us as much as you needed, as often as you needed, and about any topic. The accountant might worry about endless calls, but that's not the target market. If you are trying to make it easier for busy small businesses to select you as their accountant, the right prospects would be firms that are too busy running their business to make much use of the service anyway until they have a need. When they are able to call with a question instead of waiting until the concern has become a crisis, the accountant delivers greater value and provides a recurring revenue stream. A prospective customer might worry about signing up for a commitment of $1,000 a month if he has never spent that kind of money on the company's accountants before. Still, the right target customer would say, "That's a no-brainer, as I spent about $15,000 with my accountant last year, and I was always afraid to call her." This becomes a win-win package for that perfect prospect and the accountant. The customer now has predictable costs.

The accountant doesn't have to clean up an end-of-the-year mess since the customer has been getting advice in one- to twenty-minute increments throughout the year. The customer has access to the support he needs, and the accountant has predictable recurring revenue.

**Competing with yourself instead of your competitors**

People want to be able to pick up what they need and move on. Put your product or offering into a package. Offer multiple options so that they don't have to go somewhere else for an alternative, and carefully measure your results and refine the package until you see it performing as expected. If you have multiple options, you should already have one you think is the best value and put it in the middle. When you see most of your customers picking up that package, you are succeeding. If everyone picks up your premium package, you are underpriced. If everyone buys your value package, you are either overpriced or focused on the wrong market. If you understand your market and have reasonably divided your options, 80 to 95 percent of your customers will pick the middle option. This shows you that some can afford your "Cadillac" offering, and some can still make it in your door wanting to try something you are offering without ordering the top of your line.

Let's discuss the concept of offering multiple options and how to compete with yourself for your customers' sake. I learned this lesson when we had customers select another vendor for a project we were sure we had won, but we realized that if we didn't present options, the customers weren't sure they were making the right decision. And since we didn't have a trust relationship yet, the customers felt they needed to check out our competition to make the right choice. So we put a new rule in place. Our engineers already had to help the salespeople craft and approve the solutions we proposed to our customers. But now, every proposal had to include three engineer-approved options.

The first option was to be the minimum amount of product and service necessary to meet the exact problem the customer had described, even if this low-end solution offended our engineers' sensibilities. This option was called "good." This led to numerous and spirited internal arguments, as our engineering team didn't want to call these options good even though they were. The second option was the one that we thought was the reasonable middle ground. It was good enough that the engineers would be happy, but it still focused on being as economical as possible while providing minimal redundancy, scalability, or future readiness. And finally, the one the engineers loved, since they got to design the perfect solution as if money were no object, was the "best" option.

While many on our team complained about this new policy for the first few months, we began to see very positive results. We often submitted proposals that would take a few months to get a customer's approval, but we were losing far fewer projects. We were now competing with ourselves instead of our competitors.

### Hunters and farmers

Hunters go out and find opportunities, and they like doing it. They don't mind the cold. They don't mind unfamiliar territory and uncharted fields. In fact, they love it.

Farmers like to tend familiar fields and care for animals they often know by name. They enjoy patiently working the fields to see if they can get a better harvest this year than last year. They enjoy tracking the details and minding the calendar. Farmers prefer routines. They prefer the familiar. They excel at managing resources. They are friendly and patient.

Hunters will find you new customers. Farmers will take care of those customers.

If you are a sales team of one, you probably resonate with one of these descriptions over the other and realize that you need to learn to be both. Or you can find a partner or employee with the missing attributes. As you grow a real sales team, avoid the common mistake that business owners make, which is thinking that they can hire people who can be and *enjoy* being both hunter and farmer. Those people do exist, but they are rare and expensive. Figure out which one you need, and hire the right one. If you hire a hunter, get out of his way when he brings in a deal, and let him get back out there to find another one. If you hire a farmer, don't tell him to spend his day making cold calls. That's not who he is.

**Never forget the basics!**

Sales fundamentals from Al Slade, a friend and expert on selling:

1. Don't ever get between your prospect and his lunch or an important meeting.
2. Family references ARE important, particularly your second, third, or subsequent calls. For example: "How is Crystal's broken arm coming along? Is she okay?"
3. Never sit down before the client sits down.
4. In a first meeting, always offer to shake hands.
5. Always make eye contact when talking or listening.
6. Take the time to observe what your prospect has built. When opportunity permits, comment favorably on something you might genuinely admire.
7. Match the mood. The manner in which the buyer behaves will give you an idea of how you should

behave. Don't overdo it—he will still assume you are a polite and informed salesperson. Don't out-yuk a comedian. Don't out-enthuse a sports fan. A serious business mood by the buyer is a hint. Take it.

# LESSON #7

# VIGOROUSLY DEFEND PROFIT

If you can't see a direct path to making a healthy profit, not only will you end up out of business, but you will also fail the people who are depending on you. You should never build a business model based on losing money, hoping to make it up through volume or through growth once the market finds out about you. Using loss leaders to increase sales is one thing, but BEING a loss leader doesn't make sense. You must make a profit, or you are not really in business.

Early in the history of my first tech company, Swift Systems, I was selling DSL in downtown Frederick, Maryland. We were in an exciting position where Verizon, the local telephone company, had not yet constructed the technology required to deliver traditional DSL service, yet local demand for it was high. We had also discovered that startup companies in other parts of the country had figured out that they could rent "alarm circuits" from the phone company and a specific type of DSL modem to deliver high-speed Internet over traditional copper lines. We believed we could duplicate this locally and that it would be an excellent offering for our growing business community that needed more and faster Internet options. We had only two competitors: DSL.net from Massachusetts and a local company called ATG.

The market was in flux due to regulatory change. In the 1970s, AT&T was divided into AT&T Long Distance and Regional Bell Operating Companies or RBOCs that provided dial tone. In 1996, President Clinton signed the Telecommunications Act, which deregulated the whole Telecom Sector, permitting the establishment of a new kind of alternative phone company that could compete with the RBOCs, the local remnants of old Ma Bell.

These new CBOCs ("Competitive" Bell Operating Companies) were exciting to investors. This was a brave new model for the tired old Telecom sector, and these new CBOCs were flush with investor cash.

By the winter of 2002–2003, DSL.net was leveraging the same alarm circuit model that we were using to offer DSL services in our local market. ATG, however, was using their new and special status as a CBOC, which was protected by that Telco Deregulation Act, to resell the local phone company's more powerful capabilities at a federally mandated wholesale price point. We could not compete against that price point. ATG could now sell a service known as T1 that could reach farther, was generally more reliable, and in some cases slightly faster than DSL, for about the same price that we needed to charge for DSL. Or so it seemed.

As we began to show up on ATG's radar screen as a competitor, one of their sales reps took notice that we had beaten her out on an opportunity, and she invited me out to lunch. I suspected a fact-finding and vulnerability-seeking effort, but I was intrigued enough to take the meeting. She quickly told me that with ATG's investors and their access to the phone company's technology at wholesale costs, they would eventually beat us in every way. Therefore, I would be better off signing up for their reseller program now versus just losing to them later. I was (again, thank God) at least wise enough to ask a few questions about their business model. The answers she provided were startling and the beginning of my ability to see past the façade of a well-funded "leader-farce."

---

### Leader-farce

Markets are often dominated by entities perceived to be the leader. Consider Enron. Enron had convinced experienced analysts, institutional investors, and the market at large that it was a leader with an innovative new way to sell energy contracts to its customers at a cost basis lower than anyone else by leveraging volume and sophisticated derivatives. Other energy providers began struggling financially as they foolishly attempted to compete with Enron's new artificial price points.

With enough funding and repetitive marketing, illegitimate business and brand promises can be deployed to scare competitors right out of a market in which they otherwise believe they can compete. It is vital to be able to tell the difference between an 800-pound gorilla and a ballerina wearing an 800-pound gorilla suit.

---

### They were no 800-pound gorilla

Before I met with ATG's sales rep and after some research, I felt they were likely paying the phone company more for services than they were charging their customers. You might want to go back and read that last sentence again, because it turned out to be true! They were squandering their federally mandated advantage, feigning an even larger advantage than they actually had to help them win even more sales faster. That growth kept their investors from seeing what was really happening. They were trying to create a leader-farce, hoping to sort it all out later, and the rep had invited me to lunch to get me to give up and join them.

I asked the ATG rep how they would scale up this model if it were unprofitable. How could the company pay me a reseller commission if there was already no profit in the transaction? She looked at me angrily and dropped her fork on her salad plate. Her eyes got very intense, and she stated: "We may not make money on every deal, but we will make up for it in volume!"

I assumed there was still some venture-backed voodoo going on here that I wasn't smart enough to understand yet. Common sense told me that if they lost a little money on one customer, they would lose even more on lots of customers. It turns out common sense still works, even when you add lots of venture capital. The Telco sector soon crashed, leading to the second wave of the DOTCOM crash. This well-funded smoke-and-mirrors technique was later named "Enron accounting" as one of the infamous factors that further exacerbated recent recessions.

## Profit is under attack

The concept of profit is under attack in western society. Unfortunately, our colleges and universities have done many students a great disservice by giving them the idea that profit represents greed. I would be a fool to suggest that no relationship exists between profit and greed, but in properly governed free markets, profit is not only the fuel and reward for innovation, value, and service; it is also the lifeblood of stable economies.

You either make a profit sufficient to allow you to care for your customers, or you will fail them in some manner, even if you were the price leader. When you fail to make a profit, your competition will invest their profits to make even more by way of serving your jilted customers. This is the force of a free market, and no amount of regulation can ever replace it.

When I led my IT services business, we believed that when we sold hardware and software to our customers, we needed to have high enough margins to make sure our customers' experience was excellent. I remember one staff member, rather new to the business, who had a genuine concern that our high gross profit margins meant we were doing something unethical. However, when vendors frequently sent us the wrong or damaged items, we paid for overnight shipping to ensure the corrected item arrived without the customer's project or timeline being impacted. When we discovered a recommended item had changed materially and was no longer meeting the customer's requirements, we ordered a replacement that often cost more. This required our staff to spend time learning the new technology so they could deploy it correctly and on time.

How should these additional costs associated with going the extra mile be covered? Should we call the customer and tell him we made a mistake in his project, and it would cost him more? Should we contact the customer and tell him the vendor sent us the wrong part and he would have to pay for the additional shipping costs? If we had deployed new technology and found it was insufficient, should we tell the customer that it would cost him extra? Our customers expected us to be their guides in the ever-changing rough waters of technology. We were selling them results, and the products and services we delivered were how we did that. There are no extra fees for a guide to get you where she said she would take you, even if a detour is required. We needed to make enough profit to ensure we could get all of our customers to where we said we would take them, regardless of the obstacles we found along the way.

Technology is continually changing. The only constant in technology is change. There was no way for us to build a perfect model of operation because of this constant change.

The best we could do was to stick to a core set of technologies we knew well, keep our people trained on them, and be 100 percent committed to assuring that each deployment met the stated objectives. I am sure we failed someone somewhere along the way, but there were many times (whether people knew it or not) when it cost us dearly to do whatever we had to do to assure that our customers got what they were paying for.

### Profit should be a reflection of excellence

Hebrew scholar Daniel Lapin eloquently describes the righteousness of free markets in his book *Business Secrets from the Bible: Spiritual Success Strategies for Financial Abundance.* Lapin writes: "He who serves the best gets to serve the most." I heard him speak once, and he explained that if you provide an innovative product or service that delivers greater value to someone, you will be entitled to more customers and a higher profit! That is until someone beats you by serving those customers even better than you did.

Many believe that large companies hold some magical advantage, but I beg to differ. Service is a significant component of the customer experience, and it is available to all. A better product or service delivered by an arrogant company, disinterested in the challenges or dissatisfaction of their customers, may be able to keep the market excited by their growth, but only until the word gets out. They are losing market trust with each transaction. Market trust is tough, if not impossible, to regain. Market trust is so valuable that larger companies that have depleted theirs will buy a much smaller company at a considerable premium to acquire the more trusted company's brand name to hide their past.

Do not fear bigger competitors! Fear delivering an inferior product and service. Sell what you know your customer needs and price it appropriately to assure you can deliver it with excellence. Don't waste time figuring out how to cut costs if that means you will have to compromise your commitment to excellence. Your reputation will thank you, and so will your bank account.

### An example of the power of profit

I remember one key client's CFO who took our operations director and me to lunch, just as the economy turned downward in 2007. We had heard the CFO's company was laying off staff. I appreciated the courtesy of sending a senior executive to break the bad news to us over lunch. Still, as busy as we were—trying to figure out how to get through those difficult times ourselves—I wasn't entirely sure it was a good use of time. We had a courteous lunch that included the typical conversations about children and so forth. I began to wonder if I would have to pay for the meal since I was sure we were about to be let go. I finally broke the tension and said, "Paul, I don't mean to be brash here, but I know that you guys are in difficult times. I'm sure you've either got to let us go or cut us back, and I don't want you to feel bad about it. These are hard times for all of us, but we'll figure out how to get through." Paul looked at me as if I had just coughed into his soup.

What Paul said next has been permanently burned into my memory: "Actually, I wanted to meet with you to make sure that your team knew that we are having difficult times, but that we are also committed to keeping you paid as best we can. I invited you to lunch to ask you to work with us and not let us loose while we go through hard times." Now I was the one caught off guard! This was a company that had just let nearly half of its staff go, an established company, a company with many reasons to be proud of their significant accomplishments, and certainly much larger than ours by orders of magnitude. And they had taken the time to send a senior leader to courteously take us to lunch, reveal the challenges they were dealing with, and ask us to weather the storm with them. We had made a fair profit on almost every transaction we had with this company. That had allowed us to treat them as a most esteemed customer, and our staff knew that nothing was allowed to go wrong for them. Why? Because we could not keep our company running without the profit we received from this important customer.

Gross profit margins, often referred to by the acronym GPM, are the difference between what you pay for something (a product, a piece of software, etc.) and the price for which you sell it. My staff often just thought it stood for the idea that a healthy profit was gross. They were often concerned that we had "such high gross profit margins on all of the third-party items we sold." However, it was precisely those high gross profit margins that had allowed us to take the attitude of doing whatever it takes with this key client. Their CFO did not take us to lunch to ask us to lower our profit margins, send in cheaper staff members, or terminate the relationship. He took us to lunch to ensure that we would not cut him off from a supply line that even their board of directors had come to recognize was committed to delivering them excellence.

**Lesson Learned!**

I hope I've made the point, but I also want to be transparent and tell you that I didn't always understand the importance of this myself. When I opened my IT services business, I charged $25 an hour. I knew that the service I was offering was superior to what most of my local competitors could deliver, but I was afraid to "ask for the money." I was worried that if I charged a rate as high as my competitors, I would be taking advantage of people. After all, I had never been paid that much before as a contractor, at least not by the hour. I worried about charging too much markup on goods that I sold. I thought (and so did many who I had to shake out of this "stinking thinking" later) "they can just go online and find it cheaper, and I will lose." So as a business owner, I had to learn this lesson the hard way. The net effect was that I was paying myself less than one-fourth of what I would have made working for a company less capable than mine. I had to learn this lesson, or I would not be in business today. We had to raise our rates many times, but how much better it would have been if I had just started them at a market rate.

Get on with it and figure out how to make sure your offerings are profitable. Don't apologize for profit. Profit is noble when you intend to use it to accomplish something noble. Providing excellent goods and services is noble. So be ready to defend your profit vigorously. It is how you will fund whatever must be done to deliver excellence and keep your business growing. Excellence is what your customers want, and to provide it, you must be profitable.

# LESSON #8

# HOW TO FIND OR TRAIN PROFITABLE CUSTOMERS

You've arranged your store, filled it with inventory, sent out your flyers, advertised in the paper, announced your grand opening, and brought in the rent-a-friends from the chamber of commerce and the newspaper. Success does not arrive, however, until you finally see the public wandering in the door. What is a business without customers? Better yet, what is a business without the *right* customers? In this lesson, I want to tell you how to recognize or train profitable prospects and customers.

## The right customers will improve and grow your business

I used to think a "good customer" was anyone who could write a check for what I did. A better customer was one who also appreciated what I did. There's no better feeling than to offer your product or service to someone and have him do something along the lines of including a thank you note with your check or refer others to you and sing your praises. These are all obvious signs of a good customer, right? I wish I could tell you that were true.

A good customer often brings you expectations that border on unreasonable. They want excellent service, but they don't want to pay market rates. They frequently call you and tell you what's wrong with your services and your team and how you could improve your business to better meet their ever-increasing requirements. It doesn't always feel friendly. It doesn't always come during business hours. And to the untrained eye, it doesn't look like a "good customer."

While building my IT services company, the one I sold in 2018, I encountered just such a "good customer." When I look back at my development as a businessperson, this was one of my best customers ever. Upon hearing that I was in discussions to take on the information technology needs of this large and growing real-estate brokerage, one of my competitors phoned to warn me that several IT vendors in town had been left unpaid by this unscrupulous broker, and I'd better "watch out!" At my first meeting with this new customer, he explained that most people in "my industry" were a bit arrogant and expected to charge a lot for things that didn't work. He told me he could send a great deal of business my way and that he was influential with a significant number of real estate agents who could send us work as well, but I'd better be willing to give him preferential pricing. Off to a good start, right?

I ignored the warning of my competitor, took on this client, and the experience was awful! He complained about every single invoice we sent. He refused to pay until I would meet with him and explain what we had accomplished. He critiqued the way our engineers dressed. He complained that we didn't leave notes for his people to let them know that we had made changes to their computers, even though they had asked us to make them. He felt the amount of time we took to do various jobs seemed too long, even though he had no idea how long it should take. Meeting with him to go through a stack of invoices and attempting to explain what we had done to warrant each one so that we could get paid got to be a weekly and sometimes even a biweekly activity. I dreaded it!

I would usually have to apologize for something that didn't meet his expectations. Or learn some difficult lesson about how we had delivered value but had then failed to present it in a way that a layperson could easily perceive. I had to accept the bitter fact that we had failed to deliver the value we had claimed in some cases.

While I was often emotionally exhausted dealing with this demanding customer, it became clear to me a few years later that he had a more positive influence on our business than I realized. He helped us see that if our engineers were technically excellent but presented poorly, they would lead untrained observers to wonder if we had sent inexperienced or incapable people to work on their critical problems. He had exposed the areas in which we didn't know we were weak. He taught us that the high value we delivered when we performed our services was incomplete if, when our invoices arrived a week or two later, we didn't clearly represent the value of the work performed.

**Improve your CX**

What we had to learn was this: Serving our customers was not only about delivering the goods or services they requested; it was also about ensuring they recognized the value we had provided. We needed to understand that from the moment they first called us up to the payment of the invoice (not just receipt of it), they needed to feel good about the entire experience.

I remember returning to the office from those meetings with my real estate broker nemesis feeling exhausted and unappreciated. But I also remember putting new procedures in place, crafting new policies, and training my team to do things in a certain way so that I wouldn't have to attend those same meetings ever again! I didn't realize that he was teaching me how to transform the delivery of technology services for the better.

I began to provide my team with a standard script on how they should answer the phone, because he complained about that. I ordered uniforms to ensure that my well-trained engineers looked every bit as competent as they were. I created forms that our engineers were required to tape over the screen of any computer they had serviced to inform the user or users that we had worked on it while they were away and what had been done. We reminded them of such basics as: "You might need to change the username because I was logged into your computer while resolving your network issues."

> **Our toughest client was teaching us about customer experience (now known as CX) before that was the buzzword it is today.**

Our most challenging, most thankless, most critical, most demanding client was actually the one who helped refine us and pointed us toward much greater success. He was not disrespectful to my staff. He raised his concerns appropriately and waited to have them addressed. When I addressed those issues and made changes, he knew he had a good vendor. Thank God that while the experience often intensely frustrated me, I needed this customer's business too much to get rid of him, and then, with the benefit of hindsight, he turned out to be a *great* customer and eventually even a great friend. The confidence he ultimately had in us translated to him introducing us to a larger company to which he later sold his brokerage. He was then helping to lead that company as part of their newly expanded management team. The amount of work that he brought our way in the twelve months after his company's sale was nearly ten times what we had done for him in the prior year. There are downsides to the story as well, and as painful as they may have been, they do not diminish the point I want to convey here: Your most challenging customer may very well be your best customer.

**Identifying bad customers**

How do you recognize a bad customer or client? Typically, one might describe a bad customer as someone who complains a lot or is difficult to work with. I hope I have already dispelled that perception. Of course, there are cases when this description is accurate. However, there is a significant difference between a problematic customer trying to buy and pay for what you claim to sell while holding the bar high and a disrespectful customer. If you are not earning a customer's respect, you shouldn't get angry if they are disrespectful since you are probably only getting what you deserve. Instead, I want to contrast my real estate broker customer who would meet with me to raise his concerns and work through them against a bad customer who simply refuses to pay, doesn't allow you to respond to problems, or abuses you or your staff. As the leader, if you won't defend your people or your firm as a whole against abusive customers or clients, you will eventually lose both the clients and your employees.

A bad customer has no interest in working things out with you. A bad customer wants to dominate you and sees your business as a vending machine to be shaken until the desired item falls out without depositing any money.

**The formidable Victoria: Saying "no" can make you money!**

There is a legendary character among the leadership team at HighGear, and she is known as "the formidable

Victoria." Victoria crossed our path years ago and taught us much. She represented a giant federal contractor interested in the workflow management software we were still in the midst of building. While our staff, client base, sales, and capabilities were growing nicely, we were doing it all without any outside investors and with exceedingly light cash reserves. We were in no shape to be turning down any opportunity, or so it seemed.

Let me draw you into a conference call with her that everyone involved has found unforgettable. Much like a frustrated mother who has had it with her children, Victoria said in an incredibly sharp tone, "Look! I'm talking to you about a potential billion dollars–worth of work over ten years!" As I stared at the speakerphone on my desk with a look of skepticism, our director of finance, Carl Casserly, sat across from me. Carl was doubling as our first presales engineer for HighGear and has since become a company partner, leaving behind his focus on finance. He now helps prospective clients prove for themselves that they can do what we claim they will be able to do. But in the dual role he held at the time, split between finance and presales, Carl knew only too well how badly we needed one billion dollars–worth of anything! He showed his consternation quite visibly as Victoria scolded me for being foolish and not giving her company the free work, demanding it as proof that we could solve their technology problem. This, as she described it, was "a reasonable entrance fee into this exciting opportunity."

Victoria had explained that we could be the perfect fit for their client's very critical and timely need, but then she added, "Here's the thing, Vaughn. My director told me to say that if you want a shot at this relationship, you will send your people down here for free to help us analyze the problem and install the first prototype. And there isn't going to be an invoice. Period!" I believed she could deliver whatever she promised. She was at once one of the most powerful communicators with whom I had ever interacted and someone who appeared to be wielding the most significant opportunity we had ever been offered. It made following my instincts extremely difficult. I know that bad clients and prospects can be turned into good clients and prospects through a bit of training, while others can also be turned into monster clients and prospects via poorly thought-through concessions.

I mustered the courage, and it was as if I had to use every muscle in my body to get my mouth to open and say "No." Then I took a deep breath and added, "If you expect us to do something for free now, how much worse is it going to get when the relationship scales up? If you don't respect us now, you won't respect us later." There was an awkward moment of silence as Carl sat across the desk from me with a wide-eyed look on his face resembling someone watching a horror movie.

Finally, Victoria spoke again, and my instincts sensed she was looking for weakness. She spoke Carl's name with a question mark in her voice. "Do you know what just happened, Carl?" She quickly added, "And do you agree?"

Carl sat quietly and looked right at me without saying a word, but his facial expression and body language said it all. We needed that money! With sadness in his voice, Carl responded to Victoria and said, "Yes."

This was the moment when we realized how impressive Victoria really was. She said, "Carl, you should write this down. You just gained an important life lesson." She paused for a moment and then added, "'No' will make you money!" She left a pause in the air like a southern preacher. It allowed what she had just said to sink in. That phrase has echoed throughout our office for years. It is a powerful nugget of truth, and it is another critical point that I hope you take away from this book. Some bad clients and prospects have the capability of becoming good clients and prospects, but only if you are willing to stand up for yourself when they are proving to you that they are not acting like clients or prospects at all. When someone asks for terms that turn you into a bondservant, a flunky, or a sucker, remember that *"no" will make you money!*

Now, here is the end of the story. Victoria confessed that her director said that they needed us too badly not to pay us. He had also told her to give it her best shot to get us gratis before she told us that they were willing to pay. Victoria finished in a friendlier tone, saying, "So how soon can you get somebody down here?" We never forgot it. "No" will make you money.

If you don't respect what you do or sell enough to place a value on it, then don't be surprised when you struggle to convince anybody else. When it comes to the essential things in life, the things we feel deeply about, there is a level of passion that people can hear and see in many nuanced ways.

**I'll donate my work**

Sometimes in the early stages of building a business, we think that donating our work to another commercial entity is a good idea, the kind of one-sided relationship I've described above. We believe that while "this prospect" doesn't value our work enough to pay for it now, we will soon have this job added to our business résumé, and that will help us later. While there may be some merit to this belief, the flaw is that it rarely works in commercial business. If the owner of one commercial entity hears you donated your work to another commercial entity, he might just be willing to let you do the same thing for him! Then there is the issue that other commercial entities will not believe you were selected because of your firm's unique attributes or value proposition, but because you were free. Besides, after essentially convincing a commercial entity's decision-makers that your market value was zero on your last project, they may be more than glad to apply that same value to your next proposal as well. They may even spend your money paying someone else to double-check your work. If your inspector is a competitor, do you think he will find anything wrong? Of course, he will! Now you find yourself with an incomplete project, where the efficacy is in question and the reference or hope of one is gone, and you will have spoon fed your competitor your lunch.

On the other hand, if you have packed enough resources to be able to do this to build your business, consider donating your goods or services to an organization that traditionally receives donations, namely, not-for-profit organizations. They typically have minimal budgets and are in the business of saying "thank you" when they receive valuable assistance. They are usually very excited to be a reference for you.

However, you need to keep in mind that commercial entities still may lack enthusiasm regarding references from organizations where your goods or services were donated, if those are the only references you can present.

### Growth makes what you do more valuable

Our best clients have been very tough on us and have made many demands. We rose to the call and made ourselves more valuable than when we walked in as an unproven vendor. Therefore, we are now worth more. As employers, we know that our staff members will be looking for raises as their value grows. After negotiating with our employees and rewarding them for their increased value, one cannot fear asking the customer for a raise or initiating a conversation. You must respect yourself enough to value what you do and to believe that you are worth investing in through a tough conversation like this so that your firm can grow, especially since that growth will make what you do more valuable.

If you build a business that makes a 10 percent margin and the next year you give your staff members 6 percent more but offer your services at the same price, you are collapsing your business. Your best clients want you to continue to grow and respond to their increasing requirements. If they are running profitable businesses, they want their businesses to grow and become better as well. They want your business to operate better and satisfy their growing needs. As one of their critical vendors, you play an integral part in delivering their "better." Will you provide the same level of service you did last year? Are your products continuously being improved? Are you training your people to provide better and faster experiences for your clients? If you're not doing any of those things, you are not growing, and maybe you don't deserve a raise. But if you are doing those things and are afraid to ask for more money, you will eventually fail your clients because you will not have the resources necessary to grow with them. Now they will have to waste time and money interviewing firms to replace you.

Explain this to your great clients, and they will understand and negotiate with you, come to a win-win solution, and continue to pay you enough to be great clients. Mature firms, the ones that make great clients, want to pay you enough money so you will be excited every time they call. Yes, they have budgets, but what good client would not be willing to pay a slight premium for a continuously improving service?

We all want to get a great deal, but none of us wants to be "that client"! If you get such a great deal that your vendor feels as if he is volunteering his services, he will eventually be less excited about giving you priority. Since you are not only a vendor to someone, but you also have vendors, won't you be open to reasonably increasing the compensation of your vendors if they are reasonably increasing the value they deliver to you as you grow? I hope the answer is yes. If you want to take good care of your best clients, make sure you have the conversations necessary to keep them feeling like your best clients. Some practical things to consider are asking for automatic renewals and increases and making sure you have written agreements in place. Taking the time to put the details of your arrangement into written form will not offend a great client or a great vendor. It's your first step to resolving issues that may arise later.

### Growing faster when you are not ready is not really growth at all

Sometimes great clients will bring you opportunities that are too large for you to handle. You understand the requirements, and you may even be aspiring to those kinds of deliverables. However, if you're not sure that you can fulfill a client's needs, growing faster than you have the ability to grow is a perfect way to turn great clients into bad clients, to become exhausted as a vendor, and to fail.

If you are not quite up to the challenge, it's best to let the client know up front that you are concerned about delivering what he is asking for. A wise client might augment your services with those of another vendor. Yes, that vendor could become a competitor, but it was always a potential competitor. The difference now is that if it helps round out your product, offering, or service enough to make the project successful, you will have grown even more as a vendor, showing that you can work with others to assure you meet a customer's expectations.

If you are already in a difficult situation with a customer who has stretched your capabilities to the limit, meeting with the client and confessing that you're struggling to meet all of her expectations will usually be well received. Honesty is the best policy as you work with her on a solution and get in front of any negative repercussions. When the client sees that you put her interests ahead of your own, you will have gone up another notch in the eyes of that client. Remember, a great client is one who knows there will be issues and wants to know she can trust you to work through them as you do everything you can to meet or exceed her expectations. The best thing you can do is grow in controlled ways. The second-best thing you can do is partner with your customers to manage the difficulties of growth when you confront them.

### The 80/20/10 Customer Rule

Another thing I had to come to terms with, after failing at it many times, is what we came to call "the 80/20/10 customer rule." That is, if you have 20 percent of your customers using 80 percent of your resources, they will typically also only comprise 10 percent of your income. On top of that, after derailing you for extended periods, they will likely even disparage you after they leave, despite your every effort to address their ongoing concerns. Don't confuse these kinds of customers with "tough customers," since tough customers are demanding, but if you meet their demands, they will also reward you.

In my IT services business, there were two large medical practices. One was delighted with our service, but at one point, we had to make some staffing changes that coincided with two technology challenges that the practice was facing. The issues were unrelated to our actions or changes. One of the challenges had to do with the practice's phone system. Then there was a problem with a new version of software the practice relied on. The users did not understand that these events were not related to our staff change. It was a natural correlation since "our IT provider [us] sent in someone new, and now we have IT problems where we never had them before, so that must be the cause."

We were now doing twice the work while receiving half the praise as before and double the complaints. This was a large account that we did not want to lose, so I directed my senior leadership team to focus on their issues for thirty days. When the problem had not been resolved, our COO and I met with the client directly. It was a tough meeting. We discovered that there were areas where we had been dropping the ball, which had exacerbated the original issues unrelated to us, so it would have been an inopportune time to try to educate them on our "victim status." We made a commitment to do whatever it took to turn the account around. We succeeded, and as a result, the client increased the monthly spending significantly. Our good customer had turned into a tough customer, but they were a tough customer and not a bad one.

That was good for us. It helped us further grow our processes internally, preparing us to continue doing better work for them and others in the future.

The other firm, a slightly larger medical office, seemed to have a new complaint every day. No matter how much senior attention or time we invested, we made no perceivable progress. There was no pattern and no discernible failure on our part. And worst of all, as we identified issues, the customer would not allow us to implement any of our advice to resolve the root causes. That's frustrating since we cared passionately about delivering excellent results. It was also demoralizing for our staff to be held accountable for adverse outcomes and to also be unable to make the suggested changes. After some analysis, we discovered we were putting twice as much time into this account as we were into the one I mentioned above. However, we were charging them only $0.60 on the dollar compared to the other medical practice.

There were many indicators that this second practice was a "bad customer." The owners would not set up or follow through with meetings to ascertain and correct the situation, and they would not take our advice. When we called to collect bills that were generally not paid on time, they would ask for a discount because of something they had been frustrated about unrelated to the services listed on the invoice. I will confess that we could've done some things better. Still, unlike tough customers who either told us where we were not meeting their expectations so we could address them or simply fired us (and either can be useful), bad customers would tell us they were frustrated and were unwilling to co-invest time or resources into a solution. This is a cultural problem!

In the end, our solution was to propose a fee structure high enough to allow us to do our part of the work and theirs, and to give them a reasonable timeframe to decide. As you might imagine, they exited the relationship. This might seem negative, but it was not. We did not leave the customer hanging; we allowed them to keep their dignity, and we showed our staff that we would not allow them to be abused. In the end, we became more profitable despite our concerns about losing revenue, because we shed a burden far heavier than the reward and lifted the morale of our team.

When a person, team, or company expects results to be magical, it will be challenging to meet those expectations. If you are told that a prior vendor was "terrible," but no specifics are articulated, this should be a warning signal that you may be about to become the next "terrible vendor."

Consider asking your prospect when things began to go downhill or if he told the prior vendor about his frustrations and what responses he received. If you do not hear about substantial efforts to resolve unmet expectations, this is at least a yellow flag. Yes, bad vendors deserve to be fired, but a mature organization will quickly approach the vendor's senior leadership, articulate concerns, and demand better results. If the prospect's response feels like a lot of arm flailing, angry emotions, unspecific accusations, and high levels of drama, you would be wise to see if you can train this customer before taking him on. If he is unwilling to be trained or to learn how to be a good customer, then at some point, you will be the next vendor about whom his arms will be flailing while he talks to one of your competitors.

**Customers who never get better**

If you are doing all that you can to better understand and deliver on a customer's expectations, but there is no path to satisfying him and being remunerated fairly for that effort, it's time to cut him loose. If you are *not* dropping 10 percent of your customers each year, you are probably doing something wrong.

We started "pruning" customers in about 2015. I had long believed that pruning customers would cost us too much and that we needed to keep every customer we had. Boy, was I wrong! We could see that certain customers cost us a lot to maintain and made it challenging to generate a profit. Honest analysis would also show us that we had either sold them a vision well beyond our ability to meet their expectations or had failed to listen to or understand what they were expecting. Sometimes we had just taken on a "bad customer" without ever training him on how to become a good one. When you get to the point that you realize you've made one of these errors and that your best efforts are not producing different results, it can be a challenge to contemplate cutting a client loose. However, once we began to make some of those changes out of sheer exhaustion, we suddenly realized we had regained a great deal of time. The morale of our team improved, and the sense of hopelessness was eradicated. When we fail to contemplate the cost of an unprofitable effort, the highest price is not the fact that the employee is frustrated and disheartened; it is that the employee confronts the next good situation scared and discouraged. So do what you need to do—what you must do—with a bad customer! The yield in productivity gains will have you wondering why you waited so long.

### Before you cut a customer loose

You can work through issues with some customers. You will help each other grow. Long-term relationships are hardly ever perfect when it comes to meeting all expectations. That is not reality.

Because communication is not always perfect, even the best-communicated expectations are rarely understood as well as we would like, perhaps especially when it comes to new relationships.

When it comes to misunderstanding, a resolution is possible for parties willing to continue communicating. Even when it comes to deception, there may be some hope, but that's more difficult since it involves a personality change. I have never personally seen that happen without the influence of a higher authority, either the Creator of the universe or a judge. Clear, candid, and open communication provides the mechanism for clarifying expectations. As good vendors, we will hear the message and rise to the occasion. A good customer will see the progress and gain trust.

*Before cutting any client loose, you should first try going the extra mile.*

The responsibility for good communication and problem resolution is 100 percent incumbent on both sides of any relationship. I have turned all sorts of client relationships around by going the extra mile and communicating candidly. I would first make sure we were meeting or exceeding expectations as best as I could understand them. I would also confront the customer regarding expectations that I thought were making it impossible for us to succeed and to renegotiate those expectations or our fees to make them more reasonable. There is no guarantee this will work, but it does increase the odds that if an exit is the only way to resolve the mismatch, at least it can be peaceable. In business, your reputation is exceedingly important.

Exiting well can be more important than entering well.

# LESSON #9

## MAKING THINGS BETTER

The home I grew up in suffered from disorganization. My parents probably would've described themselves as too busy to organize the things they would put down as they walked through the door. As a result, I would often observe them trying to get out the door in absolute frustration, yelling: "Where have the keys disappeared to?" Symptoms escalated when a bill, put down amid a pile of magazines, got over-looked. I can remember the electricity being shut off, and we would need to go pay the bill in person to get it turned back on. Not only could we not find the keys for thirty minutes when we needed to go pay that bill, but when we found them, the car battery that nobody had had a chance to get replaced was also too weak to get the car started. I remember my father's despair as he troubled a neighbor for a jumpstart, only to realize it was now too late to get the electric bill paid. We would end up spending the night, with winter setting in, in the dark without heat or hot water.

I am still guilty of having the occasional pile of papers on my desk in busy times. I have enough files saved on the desktop of my computer to bring out the OCD in some. Still, the lessons of my youth have led me to a firm belief that systems must be built, maintained, and energetically cham-pioned to avoid the natural atrophy of nature. This may be what led me to create HighGear, a system focused mainly on making high volumes of work easier to manage. In other words, I am in some ways thankful for all the adversity I've ever experienced, including growing up in a disorganized home, because it is often our difficulties that tend to inspire us in the most meaningful ways.

This commitment I possess to making things better as I go along has expressed itself in various ways. I have discovered that whenever I am willing to slow down enough to create a system of repeatability for the individual task I am about to do, I am almost certain to regain that invested time in short order.

Whether you are building a tool collection, an organization full of people executing processes, or a complex piece of software, the commitment to building foundational components and systems along the way will yield significant rewards as your endeavors scale up.

> *When you were a company of one, had you taken the time to build a system of organization for all you did, you would now have an easy time introducing people to that system and helping them be quickly and sustainably productive.*

This same issue can be true in your business. If you do not realize what is happening, you may misjudge your team as low performers. However, when you were a company of one, had you taken the time to build a system of organization for all you did, you would now have an easy time introducing people to that system and helping them be quickly and sustainably productive. This becomes increasingly important as your business scales. Your people must develop new systems, and they must also advocate for those systems being maintained and improved by others. This reality requires that you establish the baseline and teach your people to enhance all that you do continuously. This is not something you do once.

If you develop systems that help busy people reach maximum productivity, the temptation may arise to sacrifice the system you will need tomorrow for today's productivity. That trade-off is never worth it, and so you must forcefully advocate that employees make things better as they go. Reward them for accomplishing it. Give them recognition for fostering it. And hold yourself accountable to do the same as you continue to build your organization.

Having been self-employed for most of my life, I can tell you that well-organized and well-orchestrated operational systems are a competitive advantage. One of the areas I have developed significant expertise in is a three-fold area of process of discovery, improvement, and automation. As I began to work my way through a difficult turnaround, this was the one lesson I had already learned that helped me in many other areas. However, it also became apparent that I needed to double down and help evangelize others to do the same. The insights I have been fortunate to gain in this area have helped me build an organization that now uses technology as our medium to empower businesses and organizations of every size around the globe to realize the same kind of operational advantages, and to distribute that organizational power out into the organization. In this lesson, I will share some of my experiences that I hope will help you as you build or repair your organization.

**Process: A way to improve your results**

The software my team and I have invented, HighGear, is in what may appear to be a somewhat crowded sector. However, it is significantly differentiated from its competition because of the people it empowers.

HighGear enables non-technical business professionals to build complex process-oriented work and workflow management solutions for mid- to large-sized teams without knowing how to write code or requiring specialized IT assistance. Selling software of this kind has afforded me a fairly unique opportunity of seeing how business process can define whether an organization runs well or poorly in the eyes of its customers, employees, and business partners.

### Understanding the need and motivation to change

Our prospects typically call with a "burning platform" of some type. The "burning platform" is a metaphor that comes from Lean Six Sigma. The Lean Six Sigma program trains and certifies people as experts in the lean process concept, which has its roots in the Toyota lean system. This system aims to reduce the number of steps required to continuously achieve a desired result at the smallest levels, thereby delivering sustainable positive change at the highest levels. The "burning platform" is just what it sounds like: It is a problem that must be dealt with immediately. If you arrived at an oil rig out in the ocean that is operating just fine to tempt the extremely well-paid workers to go back to shore for no reason, they might not be too interested. However, imagine pulling up to that same oil rig when the platform is on fire. It wouldn't be too difficult to convince those same workers to board your boat for land. Most people are not excited about change unless and until they recognize they are on a "burning platform."

At HighGear, we call that our prospect's "clear first problem." The kinds of "clear first problems" that we have confronted have ranged from change management within massive scale food production operations to audit and reconciliation efforts within complex financial services organizations to back-office operations for large insurance companies and everything in between.

## Business is process

All organizations have processes. They may have arisen organically through a process we call "emergence," where there is no specific plan, just a series of incremental layers that have "emerged." This can be compared to the way a coral reef evolves. A small crustacean needs a home, and a stable rock at the bottom of moderately shallow water presents an opportunity. There was no plan, only need. People in most organizations create their processes in the same way because of need.

Sally files the client's information in her filing cabinet when it is just the two of you processing mortgages. That filing cabinet becomes your coral reef's bedrock. You know that if you look in that filing cabinet, you can get the information you need. You hire a third person who isn't completely familiar with the filing system and creates her own system to gather and archive customers' financial data. She now places this information into another filing cabinet. Add five years and ten more people, and your small organization is now that coral reef of organically developed processes built one atop the other.

These "emergent" processes are often sufficient until the organization needs to quickly hire more staff for better customer service or to increase efficiency. This is when a focus on process becomes an asset for some and a liability for others.

## The team with the best processes delivers

About thirty years ago, I read a book titled *Customers for Life* by Carl Sewell, which I highly recommend. One of the key takeaways from that book is in the chapter "Systems

Not Smiles." Sewell's premise is that a customer seeking to have his Cadillac serviced was not nearly as interested in a well-dressed, smiling service provider as he was in one who proactively noticed that his car had recently been in the shop and inquired to see if this visit was related. If the visit was related, his customer wanted to be assured that the problem would be handled appropriately. Sewell was also aware that a customer would want a service professional who took the initiative to contact him if his car would not be ready when it was promised. This required systems to help his staff deliver a professional and improved customer experience.

What Carl Sewell understood at the most fundamental level was that good process is a powerful tool. He reported that high trust between his customers and his service professionals resulted in more sales. The point I want to make here is that your customer experience is driven more by process than it is by the members of your "wonderful" team. You must have excellent people—that is a given. A team of great people empowered by great systems will have more available time to focus on continuously improving your processes. This is a classic example of the virtuous cycle. Your commitment as an entrepreneur or leader to empowering your people with the tools and systems they need to deliver a great experience to your clients is how you deliver great employee experiences and thus incrementally improve your advantage over your competition.

### The Big Bang!

Many leaders believe they can single-handedly ascertain everything their organization needs and successfully introduce a new and better plan or system. Some will succeed, but most will not. Some will claim to have succeeded over time. Still, an honest assessment would show that the organization experienced high levels of stress that caused reduced morale and productivity, resulting in employee turnover. Leaders work on fixing the flaw of their "Big Bang" and are often too busy to realize that the real cost is not lost time, consultant fees, or reputations; it is the organizational morale and the impact on their customers.

While modern systems are impressive in their comprehensive capabilities, their implementation is often referred to as a "Big Bang." The Creator of the universe was able to pre-orchestrate the arrangement of matter into a plan entirely laid out ahead of time, but humans are rarely able to do the same thing, regardless of the project's size.

### Big Bang or emergence?

Whether we are dealing with an entrepreneur or a manager in a large Fortune 500 company, these professionals often have the idea that they must be ready to fix everything before they can fix anything, and that every possible permutation must be addressed. With older technology, this held some validity. After all, if it took you three years to build an Enterprise Resource and Planning (ERP) application and you failed to account for something critical to your business, the rollout would be a disaster. However, process improvement should not be thought of this way. After watching many clients from organizations across the globe and teams ranging from ten to tens of thousands struggle or succeed with process improvement, I have developed some firmly held opinions regarding how to do this well.

ERP stands for a class of comprehensive applications that take account of and manage the various inputs and outputs necessary to run an entire organization. Initially focused on manufacturing and distribution organizations, it typically functions across verticals and serves larger organizations from the generation of items to general ledger functions.

As I mentioned earlier, work processes develop organically within an organization, much as a coral reef evolves. To improve an organization's processes, it is essential to make small incremental changes so that any negative impacts are controllable, and the positive effects can accumulate across time.

### Going to the Gemba

The Japanese have the phrase "going to the Gemba." In police work, "going to the Gemba" would entail going to where the crime occurred. In process improvement, the most valuable information regarding how a process currently operates and how it can be improved can best be ascertained by going to where the work is done. I would take that one step further and encourage an organization to empower the person doing the work to improve parts of the process. I am not suggesting that everyone working on a factory line is capable of "systems thinking" and thereby able to improve the way processes work. I am suggesting that more people in the "trenches" of an organization are capable of this than are currently being empowered to do it.

We recently engaged one of our industry's top analyst firms to complete a research project (the results of which are available for free at HighGear.com) regarding a group of business professionals who were not identified as part of the IT department. We discovered that the vast majority of them were already involved in business process improvement efforts, but they wanted to be empowered to do more. They wanted to have more control, and they were convinced they could add more value if they had the right tools and support.

**There is a better way!**

Although my current company sells software that helps organizations improve their processes, we have to resist the temptation to allow our potential customers to delude themselves into thinking: "This looks so easy. We'll be able to get our entire business mapped into this and **then** roll it out!" While entertaining this big picture dream might lead to an easy sale, we have had to train ourselves to push back. Our new client's better path is to empower the team to make numerous small, loosely fitting improvements in parallel. But I caution strongly against trying to orchestrate a "mini-bang." A mini-bang is trying to determine everything that a team does holistically in advance of deploying a new process (whether procedural or through automation or technology). The mini-bang is usually the wrong path, just like the big bang. What I have seen to be more productive is merely beginning to track the specifics.

When we do discovery work for our clients, we find that many of their key people significantly disagree about how their business runs. Most find it surprising. This is a serious surprise and concern for anyone getting ready to implement what they previously thought would be an easy change. "How do we know what the facts are?" If we have systems that have fallen short, we will often find that people have built workarounds. If we only examine the prior system but fail to examine the workarounds that made that system work, we will be missing critical data. Suppose we interview the stakeholders and find inconsistencies in their descriptions of how things get done. In that case, we have proof that we are missing data, which is usually proof that we have yet-to-be-discovered workarounds. If we work from the top down, we will also frequently discover that people are working around the shortfalls of systems and working around the misinformed directives of their leadership. The point is that most process improvement work starts from a dangerous point: missing data, inconsistent data, or flat-out bad data. So why not make the first step gathering empirical facts rather than subjective facts? The simplest way to gather empirical facts is to put a lightweight system in place to deliver facts and then measure.

### You don't have to be a process expert to get expert results

You do not have to be an expert. You just need to throw away any assumptions and start with facts. If you cut lawns, don't believe your team members when they tell you how long it takes. Get a simple application that tracks locations on their phones and run a report on the difference between their arrival time at a particular customer's site and their departure. Now you have empirical data!

You can figure out how to apply this same fact-gathering concept in your own business. You're smart enough to do that, or you wouldn't have started your business. Once you have those facts, you are already in a better starting position than most "experts." Creating simple systems to know how many lawns must be revisited because a tool was left behind allows you to develop simple incremental improvements. Incremental improvements may include adding a reminder that asks, "Have you loaded all the tools back into the truck?" The logic is the same whether your process is massive or small. Track the facts, empower the people who do the work to examine the facts with you, and give them the power to help you fix the real problems.

### Three things to consider as you get started

**Communicate early and often.** Remember, the first time you excitedly tell your people something is going to change for the positive, they will hear roughly the opposite.

So share generous amounts of information repetitively long before the change occurs, and you are far more likely to convert the detractors of the upcoming change.

**Identify your early adopters.** While there may be exceptions, I would advise never implementing a large-scale change with everyone at once. I am confident that in 99 percent of cases, better results are achieved when a pilot group is composed of those having low resistance by nature. Give them easy access to the change and its benefits, and these early adopters will encourage others.

**Be prepared to "go live."** Something is going to go wrong with your plan on the day you go live. Smother your early adopters with support, and make sure they think that it's been a great experience. When you are ready to expand your new and better plan to those who don't look forward to change, get your support group even more motivated. Those folks who have issues with change also have no time for problems, so you had better be able to resolve the problems fast.

# THE INVISIBLE HAND

Let's go down another corridor in the life experience of a terrified entrepreneur facing a crisis. To help you understand, I need to provide a bit of context. I am a legally registered gun owner. I hate to admit that I once had to get my guns out of the house for a few weeks during the worst of my personal and business challenges. There were some nights when I awoke so troubled by my circumstances and so hopeless about getting through them that I feared that I might be tempted to end my own life. If the means were close at hand, I might just have fallen for the manipulation of the enemy of my soul, the devil himself, who had been having a field day with my low self-worth and deep state of despair.

Because of concerns for my children, having suffered the loss of my grandfather to suicide, and due to my Christian worldview, suicide wasn't an option that I would take seriously in the daylight. However, there were times at night when the thoughts swirling around in my head were very dark. This was usually when I was at the edge of exhaustion and could do no more in that day to improve my seemingly diminishing odds of getting through the worst of the crises I have shared in this book.

### Learning to live transparently and relationally

If you are going to take on anything significant, it's going to be difficult. It is an insidious trap that starts in tiny increments. We open our first business, and when we are struggling to pay our bills a year later, we hope to avoid our successful friends for just a little while until things get better next month, next quarter, or next year. Then we can tell them how great things are going.

One can feel isolated when going through crises. I am getting to the point now in life where I've learned the answer lies in living transparently and relationally with others. I don't fear that kind of transparency at all now. I don't fear another downturn, although I don't want to go through one. But I don't fear it because I would never go back to that place of isolation.

Allow me to be a warning sign and say that I allowed myself to become so isolated that it made me a significant danger to myself and vulnerable to letting my family down in a far greater way than just failing in business. I think it is vitally important that if and when we confront crises, we remain connected.

For me, ultimately, it was the grounding of my relationship with Jesus Christ that got me through.

Our nature as Type A human beings who start businesses or build an empire is that many of us end up isolating when things don't go according to plan. Yet my experience tells me that almost nothing goes according to plan, increasing the temptation for entrepreneurs to isolate themselves. That means it is even more incumbent for leaders to stay connected and even more crucial to have transparent and accountable relationships with trusted peers. Such peers take similar risks and will therefore understand what our great aunts will not.

**Safety is in the light. The monsters are in the darkness.**

Find trustworthy people taking similar risks, and then be faithful when they are transparent with you. That is where you will need to go when trouble comes because it will be where you can find the answers you need.

I went into this chasm of despair in my life, thinking I was a Christian. I came out of this dark time realizing I had been an embarrassment to my claimed religion. I had a great need to be humbled and have my perspective changed because I lived a fake life, hiding the monsters in the darkness. Living a fake life is not enjoyable, and it can be very detrimental. Allowing others whom I could trust to see behind the façade to my dysfunctional life began the healing. This was when I became a real person who could be vulnerable.

**The grace of God**

This book is full of lessons that I hope will help all who read it. However, I would be remiss in implying that merely learning lessons and applying them got me through my trials. Instead, a whole series of miraculous events happened that defied logic and the standard rules of the way the universe works that allowed me to survive despite the severe and personally cataclysmic errors I made. I could write a whole book full of those individual stories. Perhaps to do that, I would need to enlist the aid of my colleague Carl Casserly, who had the misfortune of joining my business just before some of the most challenging times began. He was a blessing from God. Not only did Carl *not* give up as we went through the worst of it, in one of the most difficult hours, he even cashed in a retirement account to invest in the company, knowing his entire investment would be used to cover a single payroll and one month's office rent.

Carl is a good investor, and he was confident we would make it through and that he was actually buying in at a discount. I believe his decision was led by his belief in Jesus Christ and Christ's preeminence over all things. He was also partially compelled to help a friend, which I was fortunate to have become. The reason I would include Carl if I were to write a book just about the miracles that occurred is not just because he invested at a difficult time. Carl also became the company's finance person and experienced firsthand the myriad perils we faced and how narrowly we escaped. And it was through unexpected, unpredictable, and otherwise unexplainable occurrences. You could try to tell me that God does not exist, but you would be wasting your time.

### No option but to pray

One afternoon event I remember was Carl telling me that we needed a little over $88,100 in hand to deposit by the end of the week, or we were not going to make payroll, there would be no lights on, and we would be out of business. How's that for delightful news to carry home for the night? There were many stories like this, and I can still remember the look on Carl's face. It became an indicator of the condition of our finances. If he looked happy and healthy, we had enough to get through the week—yes, our human dashboard had gotten down to measuring safety in days! If he looked as if he had something for lunch that disagreed with him, we probably had only twenty-four to seventy-two hours of business expenses covered, perhaps less. In this situation, we had no receivables large enough to cover the need. I remember one instance when we had already asked many of our customers to pay early, and there were no outstanding sales that could be closed in time. We had no option but to pray, so we did.

Less than twenty-four hours later, a customer walked into our office, told us his company had some year-end budget left over, and wondered if he could prepay for one of our services for the coming year. The amount he prepaid (later that very day) left us with one cent over the amount that we needed for the bills we had to cover by the close of business that Friday. I can still remember Carl calling me into his office and looking somewhere between tearful and joyful. He looked at me and said, "It's like God knew exactly what we needed, and He covered us."

Carl and I both went home and told our wives about this miracle, somewhat embarrassed that God had to give us only one extra cent to make sure we didn't fail to notice the connection. In some ways, telling our spouses may have been a mistake. In times that followed when we were feeling sorry for ourselves over needing this or that by a specific date or having some new crisis, both wives would confidently remind us that God seemed to be looking out for us in the past and probably had us covered this time, too. Of course, that's not what a suffering control freak wants to hear. I wanted my misery validated and my worries to receive significant pity! But the truth is, they were right. Carl and I were both in training, and we needed to learn that despite the fact we could not trust ourselves to know what to do in tricky waters, God had already decided we would not sink.

I cannot declare that we deserved this, and it is part of why I feel compelled to share just a sample of the abundance of miracles we experienced. I only learned these lessons that I am fortunate enough to share in this book because God decided to extend grace to me despite my best efforts to ruin my business and life. Since He did the saving, He also gets the glory.

### The providence of God

After "the humbling of Vaughn Thurman," when I finally began to change, things began to improve markedly. However, in hindsight, God was certainly with us all along the way. How else would I have ever made all those payments to the Internal Revenue Service? How else would I have ever negotiated a forbearance agreement with a bank that had the right to take my house? How else would we have kept so many customers through the downturn? How else was I able to hang on to an excellent staff? How else was I able to remain married to a wonderful woman who deserved better?

What follows is a series of stories that either I or someone else in my organization deemed worthy of saving along the way that help illustrate that there was something larger going on:

### Reflection #1: The turning of the tide

We survived the worst of the economic downturn, but now we felt we were falling behind again. Many companies were beginning to recover, but we seemed to be stuck. During this challenging time, we were out of resources and with well-resourced new competitors emerging from everywhere. At the same time, I had begun to realize that I was the problem. I was not only working on radical change in the business, rooted in the radical change I was trying to accomplish in myself; I was also trying to be the savior for my team by protecting them from many of the difficulties that we faced. I believed it was my responsibility to figure out how to fix everything, and I secretly assumed they would leave me if they knew how bad the situation was.

First, it meant that people who should have been experiencing a little bit of healthy fear (the kind that I described that causes one to analyze the options and take action) were not experiencing any fear at all. I was in full panic mode, trying to figure out how to get us through crisis after crisis while leading a team that was conducting "business as usual." Second, it meant that I was desperately alone in some of the most challenging battles that we faced as a company. Not only did I not have the help of a fully aware team, but I also lacked the internal accountability for whether or not

I was making wise decisions in the face of many challenges. Third, people could tell that *something* was wrong, but they could not tell *what* was wrong.

I once worked at an organization that had shown me the cost of that last error, yet I had failed to absorb the lesson. Management would sometimes hunker down in the conference room for days at a time. The staff would assume that layoffs, a shutdown, a loss of critical customers, or all sorts of other negative possibilities were imminent. As fear escalated, some of the staff members even began updating résumés during the workday or spending company time on job boards trying to figure out where they would land next. When the management team suddenly emerged after three or four business days with exciting news, imagine their surprise when the team members didn't look excited since they had all been imagining the worst instead of planning for a bright future! The situation would have been much more productive if management had let everyone know what was happening.

Having had this experience, how could I fall into the same trap? Though misguided, I found it easier to handle problems in secrecy than to be transparent. Since I was concerned that my past business choices had led to disaster, I began to feel that sense of the chair tipping over and not wanting to call out for help because I wasn't sure that anyone would care to grab the chair in time to save me.

What I really wanted to do was to figure out how to stop falling in the first place to avoid the humiliation altogether. Besides, I was more worried about people abandoning me than I was about failure itself. When things go wrong, we should disclose early and disclose often—even to our team members.

In 2012, when I recognized that I was the problem, one of the first things I began to implement was a pay-for-performance program. I did this to educate team members on the impact their performance had, help them understand more of the management team's decisions, and see how outside forces impacted us. This was terrifying for me!

While some of our team members got scared, packed up, and hightailed it out of town, just as I feared, some of them swallowed the unpleasantness of our situation and began to focus on what they could do to increase revenues. They began to connect the dots, and we promised that as we turned the company around and made it profitable again, they would get a share. Because we knew it would be hard work, we promised that the employees would get half of the profits that we could produce for the first three years once we restored the company to profitability, and we delivered.

In March 2013, after roughly nine months of sharing bad news and brutal truths with team members who were surely wondering if they would ever see "their share" of our hoped-for turnaround, we began to see the fruit of doing things differently. The email that I share below is one that I sent out to my team while feeling overwhelmed by grace on a Good Friday. We had taken a hard risk and engaged those ablest to help (our team), but the sequence of events that led to me fighting back tears of joy on that Friday evening cannot be explained by employing new business tactics alone. As you will see in this email, it was clear that as I was beginning to accept the need to change, I was the benefactor of a gift that can be described only as Providence. There were many times when I had to recognize that God was doing what I could not, verbally and in writing. Based on the many mistakes I made, what I deserved was failure. But instead, I received grace. That is what He does! I'm glad Carl saved this email so that I can share it with you:

From: Vaughn Thurman
Sent: Friday, March 29, 2013 3:39 PM
To: All staff
Subject: A very Good Friday!

All,

I wanted to share with you just what a fantastic day (and week) it has been. We did not expect the *CUSTOMER A* proposal to be executed until June, but it came in yesterday.

We did not expect to see a 6-figure deposit check so quickly either, or for *Customer Contact D* to hand-deliver it—excited to do so, but he did today.

Today Al told me that he has new sales appointments every single day of the week next week. The three appointments I had with him on Wednesday were also exciting prospects, leading to real opportunities.

Today the very same bank that coldly rejected us and called in our loans six years ago came in and wrote us a six-figure line of credit for Swift Software ... and this has opened the doors to a new and better relationship.

Today we looked at our cash position and were astounded at the change. At the beginning of the week, we were still concerned about making payroll on time, but the amazing surprise is that we already had both companies covered (well, everybody but me, but you get it—everybody that mattered :- ) and all of this was before getting *any* of this in hand today.

Today, in one day, we have gone from fearful and wondering to remembering that God is fearsome and wonderful and that he continues to carry us through.

Our sense of excitement and hopefulness has turned on a dime for those of us close to it. On the Systems side, our marketing efforts are starting to pay off, and our long loyal customers continue to support us and trust us with increasingly large projects. On the software side, we found a bridge to help us get our massive and exciting project done without so much financial stress in the most unlikely of places—the very bank that kicked us to the curb. They told us today that they learned we were trustworthy by how we have handled these challenging years, honoring our commitments to them despite their actions toward us during the housing crisis. That had a lot to do with why we got this new credit line and why the door has opened for more if we need it.

I have often insulated all of you from the trials of running a business and making payrolls, and keeping all the wheels going, but this time I am glad I have not because it has inspired many of you to do more, to try harder, and to contemplate how interdependent we all are. This awareness lets you share in the joy with me—of seeing how exciting this turn of events is. We are busy with new opportunities. Our marketing efforts are starting to work with JobTraQ [now HighGear] back to position #2 or 3 on Google. And Swift Systems' pipeline of projects and new opportunities is also filling back up faster than ever before. On the systems side, we have proposals going out and new opportunity meetings every day next week.

I don't know where each of you stands spiritually, but on this Good Friday, I just wanted to share with you how thankful I am to see God provide for us and the part that each of you and your excellent work has played in us all getting through so many obstacles that we started this week with, together.

I send you into the weekend with this question: There is one who saved me and continues to rescue me as you have all now seen. Do you know Him? http://www.youtube.com/watch?v=yzqTFNfeDnE

And finally, it is Friday, but Sunday is coming http://www.youtube.com/watch?v=YbyT6wfdhJs

Thanks, have a great weekend, and may God bless you all!

~Vaughn

### Reflection #2: A path with different results—the fruit of seeking counsel

I was increasingly busy managing the turnaround of two companies, and I needed help. For that reason, I hired someone who had experience selling precisely the kinds of things we sold. Like David Attenborough in the movie

*Jurassic Park*, "I spared no expense!" But it was closing in on a year, and the only business this person had closed was the business that I had essentially closed for him.

When he told me that the problem was our marketing, our messaging, our product capabilities, or various other issues, I took him seriously, overlooking the fact that I had been able to sell our product despite these glaring needs. We worked on all those things for him, and none of those efforts hurt us in any way. After all, they helped us make things better, but they didn't help him produce any sales.

### I waited too long to deal with the obvious

I waited too long to deal with the obvious. He was quite convinced that I was making an error when I finally confronted him because he appeared unable to get the job done. He told me that the opportunities in his pipeline were "just about to close, probably within the next thirty days!" He was so confident that he suggested that he not get paid for those thirty days while proving that he could get these sales closed. There was a time when I might have been very excited about this kind of offer, but I was a different professional now. I was not a man who could take advantage of someone struggling with a task in which he had already proven he could not succeed.

The old me would have fired him on the spot and then badmouthed him, maybe for the next six months. The old me would have stewed about it all night and then failed to act, caught between wondering if he really had the deals and I would thus be losing out, or if I was just being hustled. But the new me called for advice. I called five other businesspeople as well as my pastor. The advice I received was excellent. I would still pay him his base salary, but only if he closed the deals that he committed to closing during that period. He would need to give me a daily report on the status of each of the deals in his pipeline.

This was not the position for him, which became abundantly clear to both of us because of the straightforward way we dealt with the situation. He and I would remain friends, and he ended up getting a job better suited for him. By thinking this through and seeking the counsel of others, I clarified the situation, developed a realistic way out that honored him, and dealt with the reality at hand. And we were able to move forward constructively.

---

From: Vaughn Thurman—Swift Systems Inc
Sent: Wednesday, July 31, 2013, 6:36 PM
To: Vaughn Thurman—JobTraQ
Subject: Thank you—and how it worked out

Thank you to each of you who are copied on this email for being an outside resource for me today, a virtual short notice sounding board of wise men if you will. I appreciate the time more than I can express. Likewise, for your advice, which was almost unanimous, to "give it a try, with some conditions."

I decided to follow the majority consensus since it was also where my head was by the end of the process anyway. The funny thing is that I would NOT have done this without making those calls. When I told him I would accept his offer (with the modifiers from my advisors), he immediately tried to renegotiate what he then called "an offer he hadn't thought through well enough." He talked for five more minutes and showed me he did not believe he would turn things around (the

---

main reason I wanted to give him an extended chance). And he hoped he could talk his way into another 30 days of base pay. The lemons rolled up in my eyes—no jackpot. I let him go.

He was surprised because he thought he had me. That revealed so much to me. I was gracious, and because a moment earlier I had been prepared to accept his offer, he thanked me for the opportunity he had, and we agreed to part amicably. It's beautiful to see how God works. If I had not sought counsel (following Proverbs' advice), I would have just let him go and always wondered if he was about to turn it around. If I just let him go, he would have been able to say, "I even offered to stay at that damn place for nothing, and they let me go." I got to take the high road, which led him to show his cards, and they were not what he had previously said. Because I had been gracious, he couldn't find fault with the outcome, and from there, it was the warmest "letting someone go" I have ever been a part of. Thank you for helping to steer me into what was God's path. I have a clear sense that this was the right outcome on many levels. The salesperson I called you about has genuinely been introduced to the Gospel while he was here, and I believe God crafted an exit today that did not undermine that for him, and that is a very good thing. Without your wise advice, I would have taken a less gracious path and would have missed out.

And a reply…

From: "D.H." [My pastor at the time—apparently prophetic!]
Date: August 1, 2013, 7:28:08 AM EDT
To: Vaughn Thurman—Swift Systems Inc
Subject: RE: Thank you—and how it worked out

Better file this story away for the time when you will write your autobiography or when you teach others about leadership. May the reigning Lord advance into this man's heart through the grace shown to him through this employment opportunity. Amen!

### Reflection #3: Learning to do the right thing, even if it costs

There is more to this following story than the email will show. However, I am glad this one got saved because it is particularly poignant. The person in this story has been renamed Suzette, a highly competent woman who led operations at one of our larger customers. Their CEO, who I have renamed Marcus, was by far a better businessperson than I, but his disposition was very similar to the old me. He would delegate tasks without a great deal of clarity, make demands without properly resourcing or empowering the people to whom he had delegated the work, and would get extremely frustrated with people who couldn't wade through all of that and deliver the extraordinary results he expected.

We supported this customer's IT team, which was beginning to fall apart. The IT leader was emotionally exhausted. Not only was she being held accountable for projects for which she was not resourced, but unfortunately she was also not quite capable of delivering them. The situation finally broke down as the IT leader gave notice. The CEO brought us in to see if my team could assess his organization's current condition. I quickly ascertained that while we could deliver a report, the need was more complicated. The CEO believed he had several people on his team who could assume the role of IT leader and help him get the company from where it was, with an underpowered IT department, to where it needed to be.

I interviewed the two most likely candidates. One was Suzette, who didn't want the job but was competent and willing if called. I developed a high regard for Suzette, an astounding "get things done" kind of professional. Intellectually she could certainly do the job, but there was no practical way she could do it. Her competence generated this dissonance as she had already been assigned to manage just about everything else in the business. The other candidate certainly had the desire and had more formal (though dated and unproven) IT schooling, but I was concerned that this person's motives were more self-serving. Suzette would serve the organization. I asked her for permission to advocate for her, and I explained what I believed would need to change for her to succeed. I was keenly aware that it was God enabling these insights. I could see problems due to the many similar errors I had made over the years leading people and managing my own business.

A while later, Suzette phoned me and asked if she could stop by to share some concerns she had before I met with her CEO. I believed I could help advocate for her getting more resources, and she did not need to be an IT expert. The things I expected to be on her list turned out not to be the real issues, and what she shared stopped time. Suzette's husband was dying.

Doctors had told Suzette that if her husband had another setback, he would likely not be around for more than a few months. Her biggest concern was that she hoped she could try to get the organization to a point where she *could* leave to take care of her husband. I asked her to imagine what she would do if her CEO had the budget necessary to hire a whole team of people to do her job. I can still see her face as she stared at the floor for a moment and then looked up and answered, "I'd buy a cabin in the mountains as my husband has always wanted, and I'd take care of him. Then I'd figure the rest out."

We talked for nearly another three hours that evening. We hardly got back to her situation at work at all. I shared my faith with Suzette. I shared some of the crises I had confronted and how God had rescued me time and time again. I shared how I had the wrong priorities for so many years and how God restored my life and perspective. Suzette's situation was complicated, and if she decided to do what she had told me she wanted to do, it would probably not bode well for us as a vendor to her company.

Nonetheless, I asked if I could pray for her. I prayed that God would give her wisdom and help her make the right choice. I prayed for her husband, and I prayed for the company where she worked. I ended the prayer by saying that I believed all of this was in God's hands and that I was willing to help any of the parties involved.

A few weeks later, when I checked in with the company's CEO, I discovered that he was too busy to talk to me because his head of operations had given her notice. He was happy for her even though he was upset. She was "getting a cabin in the mountains and was going to take care of her dying husband." He also informed me that they would not need our services now, as he had promoted the other individual who was sure did not need our help. The truth was, he needed it a great deal more than Suzette would have, and in time it showed. However, that was still the best bad news I had gotten in a long time. I would have enjoyed working with Suzette, and she would have given us a lot more work, and I believe it would have helped that company a great deal. But I can tell you that knowing I helped somebody decide to do the most important thing in her life was worth a million times all of the checks we might have gotten if Suzette had put the business opportunity first. I pray this email makes you think of someone or some situation that needs you to do the right thing for the person, even if it doesn't seem like the right thing for your business.

---

From: Vaughn Thurman
Sent: Friday, April 04, 2014, 8:14 PM
Subject: Re: Reports to?

Sometimes a simple recognition of effort can go so far for the human soul. Reading this did a bit of good for me.

The truth is, I've just been applying Jim Collins / biblical principles here—trying to avoid a failure for them. Their CEO is a lot like the old me—high energy, visionary, but gets frustrated with people quickly and doesn't have the time or knowledge to build objective measurements in this area. His future IT people need a buffer from that, someone steady and less exhausting for them since they often don't know how to solve it. Swift could offer a lot here if we could build objective measurements to bubble up to the CEO through a good people manager. And that good people manager could objectively help Marcus manage his expectations.

Plus, Suzette still likes my analogies, which everyone here at Swift has already grown to find annoying. It's just the vendor honeymoon phase! :- )

~Vaughn

From: Suzette
Sent: Friday, April 04, 2014 7:16 PM
To: Vaughn Thurman
Subject: Hi Vaughn,

Based on a conversation with Ted today, I believe he wants to pitch something to Marcus. I owe Ted the respect to make his play, and I want to see Marcus's reaction. Ultimately, I will do what is best for the company, but I have a pretty full plate and some very aggressive goals to achieve. That being said, I am 100% in agreement that a direct report to Marcus is not a good solution. Thanks for your support and very sage perspective. You don't have to care as much as you do. The fact that you are sincerely concerned about what is the best solution is appreciated—and quite impressive.

Sincerely, Suzette

From: Vaughn Thurman—Swift Systems Inc
Sent: Friday, April 04, 2014 05:42 PM
To: Suzette
Subject:

Suzette,

I believe that until you identify another candidate for such a role (executive ownership of IT), this new person (and other IT personnel) should report to you. I didn't spell out your name in my guidance to Marcus, but that is where I picture this going. Are you on the same page? May I have your permission to try and clarify the same with Marcus?

I'd like to get that done ASAP but wanted to think about it a bit more and also run it by you before approaching him with the idea.

Best regards, Vaughn

And you, the reader, already know what came next. I'm glad someone saved this email so that I could remember to tell you this story. Of all the deals I never won, I suspect this was my greatest.

### The counterintuitive ... a path less traveled

I would not have written about most of these things before having gone through a crisis. Hindsight, the exorbitant ticket price of experience, has taught me what circumstances and the obvious could not. I have instinctively resisted the cattle chute all of my life. When I see all of the "cattle" moving in one direction, my instincts have always told me that something must be wrong and I should go a different way. That often led me to the role of "rebel without a clue." Early in my business endeavors, this personality trait was valuable to steer clear of foolish fads. This same stubborn orneriness caused me to resist many things that would have also helped me as the years progressed.

The following passage from the Bible has had great significance as I have continued my journey:

> These things we also speak, not in words which man's wisdom teaches but which the Holy Spirit teaches, comparing spiritual things with spiritual. But the natural man does not receive the things of the Spirit of God, for they are foolishness to him; nor can he know them, because they are spiritually discerned. (I Corinthians 2:13–14 NKJV)

The apostle Paul was making the case here that there is a kind of knowledge that a man can have only after being connected to God. Having such experience allows one to see things that were not previously discernible.

I have to say that being born unruly, I was attracted to the idea that the world might be going in the wrong direction. There had to be additional information available to help us process the truth hidden from us. Without hesitation or doubt, I believe that there is another dimension to this life that we are not privy to unless we have become connected to God by recognizing our need for Him and accepting the free gift as offered by His Son, Jesus Christ, who died for us as a substitute for the punishment we deserve for our egregious ways. Eternal life is not just something that begins in the post-life future we once feared (without God). Eternal life begins the moment we accept the blending of Christ's spirit with our own, bringing us back into the ability to see not only the things that are plainly in front of us but also the things that were previously hidden. The Bible is full of such mystery. The person who is willing to work hard to extract the information it holds will find it the most fascinating source of learning, inspiration, and guidance.

That is also one of the sources of information that I leaned on in my times of difficulty. When my mind is in panic, I cannot trust it. Therefore, I lean on the Holy Spirit, who connects my spirit to God. God is not concerned about running out of resources and is not afraid of the future. God does not abandon His plans or His friends, and He is never caught off guard. And if I am willing, God is always ready to be my friend, mentor, and advisor. If I am on the wrong track, He will quietly tell me that it will be okay, and He'll help me find a new one. If I am on the right track, even if I don't know it, He will also quietly tell me that everything will be okay and help me find the way through. He will go with me through the entire journey, and He will help me grow to become even more of an example of grace for others to see. Thank God that His ever-present offer was available to me, as it is to you.

# LESSON #10

# THE BEST WAY OUT
# IS THROUGH!

As previously mentioned, this book is being written amidst the COVID-19 pandemic of 2020. We don't know what toll it will take on the United States' economy and the world at this point. We do know that many folks have not been able to make a living for many months. Small businesses are suffering, and many will not make it. Some have already closed their doors forever. Even leading national companies are closing stores or declaring bankruptcy.

It is the perfect time to learn the lessons discussed in this book as many of us regain lost momentum and must do so with limited resources.

Unfortunately, it takes situations like this, a global crisis, to get our attention. Talk about stubbing our toes on large pieces of furniture in a dark room! COVID-19 is one very large, oversized Victorian breakfront.

I serve (as often as I can) on an advisory board that supports entrepreneurs in a local incubator and, as the crisis began, I experienced a disturbing trend. In one of the first sessions that the group held after the beginning of the pandemic, the advisors as a nearly unified group began suggesting that some of the entrepreneurs essentially "abandon ship" and go after whatever opportunity seemed to be presenting itself as a part of the crisis.

The suggestion was made to someone to scrap his current efforts and work on producing hand sanitizer. This didn't trouble me because it was a bad business suggestion in general. After all, if lots of consumers want hand sanitizer, that means there is demand. And, depending upon the number of suppliers, there could be at least a short-term opportunity. However, what disturbed me was the suggestion that people who either had or were building otherwise viable long-term business models should scrap them to chase what everyone knew was a short-term, crisis-generated opportunity.

**When times are difficult, there are many reasons to quit**

When times are difficult for a business owner, there are many reasons to quit. Instead, we must learn to handle short-term pressures and risks and balance them, keeping potential long-term rewards in mind to talk ourselves into staying the course. Unfortunately, our ability to approach situations like this while keeping the long view in sight does not improve with experience unless we do it. These kinds of challenges will confront us repeatedly. If we do not learn how to handle them, we are likely to repeat them.

Sometimes those "reasons to quit" are valid. There is no use in deluding ourselves if we are at the end of the road. But we need to be judicious. Our minds are tremendously capable of imagining catastrophic "what-if" scenarios that lead to our unrecoverable demise when we assess the long view, especially at night. Add to that a dose of the evening news before you head to bed, especially in troubling times, and it is easy to spend the night contemplating the certainty of our failure. This is a weight that most will never fully understand until they have risked their own fortunes, reputations, and futures on something that is exceedingly hard to accomplish and then finding themselves with good reason to wonder if they will accomplish it at all.

It's no wonder we are tempted to abandon course when trouble comes. However, the correct response to disturbing circumstances beyond our control is to slow down and evaluate all the information available before making our next move.

## Preparation for crisis

I heard a talk by a former officer in the Special Forces on the value of responding to crisis deliberately. He said that recruits were a vulnerability to themselves and others in their squad despite their intensive training because they had no experience on the battlefield. For this reason, he would work aggressively to get them to understand that if they heard gunfire, regardless of the fear and helplessness that might overtake them, they were to drop to the ground, seek cover, begin evaluating the situation, and be ready to report. He described an incident in Afghanistan when his men were suddenly confronted with gunfire. Fortunately, his men knew what to do. They dropped to the ground and began listening and counting. He began to call out names to find out if all the members of his team were alive. He then began seeking reports from his team regarding the number of hostiles they believed were shooting at them as well as the general position of the adversaries. He had trained them to prepare their ammunition, position their rifles, and verbally report the enemy's positions, so that when they responded, they would be responding as one team, attacking the enemy positions together.

Consequently, they made quick work of a hostile force twice their size. During the period of silence after the initial ambush, the enemy believed they had either killed their opposition or had them pinned down. This underestimation cost them their lives. Had these Special Forces members not been adequately trained before this incident, they might have fired back aimlessly and been picked off one by one. The outcome would have been very different.

Similarly, when we enter a business crisis, we may experience all sorts of emotions. Fear, for example, while helpful when it alerts us to danger, can also paralyze us or cause us to run from non-threats. Our natural response as humans seems to let our lower instincts take over and demand urgency. It leads businesspeople to make bad decisions. If your response mode has kept you from effectively dealing with a serious problem in your business, you will still have that serious situation. You will have failed to take advantage of the transformational opportunities that exist in upheaval. That opportunity is to take the road less traveled and press through the crisis, making your product, service, or offering more valuable or relevant.

**Responding to crisis**

Early in the pandemic, the governor of our state, like the governors of many other states in the country, issued a lockdown order. "Nonessential" businesses were closed, and residents were ordered to "shelter in place." Similar orders were issued around the world. Reality was changing fast! One of the immediate results within our company was that our new prospects virtually vaporized.

One of the early effects was a sudden and significant downturn in the stock market, and several of those prospective customers were very large-scale investment firms. They needed us more than ever, but they were in crisis. They were no longer examining the long view; they were focused only on the here and now.

The intuitive reaction to our crisis might have been to start reducing headcount. Many CEOs I know began bracing for the worst and building spreadsheets detailing how they could get through without half their staff. We were running at a structural loss before the crisis. I had started the year having hired up and increasing various expenses so that we now needed to grow the business by another 80 percent to get back to break even. I certainly had the temptation to pull out the axe myself and begin chopping down pieces of the house that didn't seem necessary in a crisis. However—and I do not by any stretch claim that I did not experience uncertainty, panic, or urgency—I allowed myself the time so that I didn't make bad short-term decisions. I created a process that included monthly board meetings and a deadline.

If we could not figure out how to improve things within three months, we would take the necessary action and cut costs. The impending deadline motivated us to think strategically and figure out how to improve our situation.

In parallel to our new customer pipeline drying up, several of our existing customers did some downsizing, and some closed their doors forever. Various government programs, including the Paycheck Protection Act, slowed this trend. Still, if things didn't improve when those funds ran out, many CEOs were sure that downsizing was inevitable and necessary. We were only a few weeks into the crisis, and if I had allowed myself to make strategic decisions on any of those worst days, I certainly would have done long-term damage, and it would have been unnecessary. I put out a policy statement in the first few days of the lockdown stating that our response would be reasonable, rational, and measured. And I held myself to it even when I felt like doing something rash.

Here is that policy statement that went out to staff, customers, and vendors:

Freedom, a Rational Response, and Confidence

A Message from Our CEO—Our Response to the Coronavirus

Responding to the Unexpected

So how do we respond to the unexpected while the unexpected is still happening? How do we plan and move forward when each day delivers more uncertainty instead of less? I've put a few thoughts together to tell you how we are dealing with these things at HighGear, and why we believe our new normal may not be so abnormal after all. In fact, it may even be an opportunity to shine.

I feel very fortunate to lead a team of people at HighGear who naturally prioritize meeting others' needs. They are a brilliant, focused, and cohesive team. They even laugh together, frequently. Their commitment to serving our market was reflected late last week by somebody saying, "Vaughn, your team has always gone above and beyond. I mean it; every one of them has a servant's heart." This same person's boss confirmed the sentiment a few hours later, unaware of the previous communication.

Honestly, it was a needed ray of sunshine amid a pretty stressful week. This may not come as a surprise to any of you who have interacted with them, especially recently, as they continue to be a wellspring of joy and service, but they are also just human beings like the rest of us. They are fathers with families, young people with their whole careers ahead of them (at HighGear, of course), new team members eager to make their mark, immigrants, hobby farmers, serious nerds, gamers, avid fishermen, and I could go on. But we have this one driver in common: We all want to do the right thing.

Critical Question

Let me risk giving an overly simple answer to a complex question by saying that the right thing to do in troubled times is the same thing to do in easy times: The right thing!

We can't serve clients if our first thought in a crisis is "What's in our best interest?" because we will immediately have a conflict of interest. If we remove fear, then what's next? Hopefully, the rational response will be to recover from whatever had us afraid and shift toward empathy. We can help a customer, a co-worker, a vendor, or a friend when we see they are in need, even if it costs us.

Mother Teresa said, "I have found this paradox, that if you love until it hurts, there can be no more hurt, only more love."

Our Framework

We have a responsibility to our staff's well-being, to meet our clients' needs, to succeed for our shareholders, and to be decent to our vendors. Within that framework, there is never a conflict of interest because serving the stakeholders who support us IS how we succeed.

It isn't that we are altruistic, though we certainly aspire to get as close to that as we can. It is the realization that doing the right thing when storms come can genuinely enhance our ability to succeed once they pass.

We don't sell technology at HighGear; we sell value. Isn't that true for you as well? If our products and services are good and our commitment to delivering ROI is excellent, we can earn our market's trust, their referrals, and the opportunity to serve them more over time. But these high ideals aren't proven when things are easy; they are verified when the stakes are high, and it costs us something to deliver what we say we aspire to. The point here is—this is your time to shine too!

In times like this, it pays to inspire and empower your people to do the right thing for others and to keep the rules simple so the decision-making can be timely. We want our team to be ready to give a rational response and to be confident that they have the freedom and support to do the right thing.

Our simple rules for uncertain times:

We trust our team with the Freedom to: 1) adapt to the changing needs and realities of our marketplace, and 2) work through challenges as professionals.

We stay well-informed of the situation and regularly communicate to be counted on for a Rational Response.

We will not overreact, nor will we fail to manage our risks.

We will have confidence getting through trouble because we have experience overcoming adversity and working with trustworthy and empowered people committed to doing the right thing.

Our confidence doesn't mean that we believe there won't be difficulty. It doesn't mean we think we can glibly ignore risks or avoid impacts. Instead, it means that we think that with a great team empowered with the freedom to act and committed to a rational response, we can have confidence in our ability to find a way to get through trouble together.

We are committed to serving our marketplace to the best of our abilities, regardless of the situation.

So, what's the right thing to do in troubled times? The same thing we should always be doing: The right thing.

That's HighGear's Golden Rule.

We'll be there for you in the same way we genuinely hope you'll be there for us once trouble has passed. But it's not quid pro quo. It's just the way we roll.

Sincerely yours,

Vaughn Thurman CEO, HighGear

Forgive me as I state the obvious, but there is nothing more dangerous than a leader in panic. Consider when politicians feel the pressure of "somebody has to do something!" Fearing the prospect of being held accountable for inaction, politicians often run into the fire with no real plan, urgently throwing our future earnings at the problem as foolishly as if they were throwing money into a fire, hoping it would act to suppress it.

When a crisis comes, slow down, think long term, and then act rationally.

**It was time to raise our price!**

You might ask what would lead us to think, with our pipeline drying up and customers canceling services, that raising our price was the right thing to do? We had felt for some time, even before the crisis, that we had been underpriced. We knew that some prospects had worried that our product couldn't be as good as we claimed, considering how little we charged. However, we had been afraid to raise the price and risk hurting our pipeline's flow rate. Now, *we had nothing to lose*. We could experiment with what the market would bear using the few leads coming in. We knew that none of those leads would be enough to solve our revenue problem, but if we could get our pricing correct, perhaps it would help in the future. In the end, after much market research (that we now had plenty of time and human resources to accomplish since we were slow), we decided to double our price right in the middle of a crisis.

As we began to share the price increases with our customers, some said, "Oh, no!" Some said, "I figured that was coming eventually. You haven't changed your prices in the eight years our company has been with you." And some said, "Your product would still be worth every penny if you were five times as much, but it's going to take me some time to get this approved. Can you work with us?" One even shared that the previous year his firm's technology committee had stated that he should find a way to lock us to the current price because the price was "too low" for what we were offering. We were selling to titans of industry, and we had been scaring some of them away by undervaluing our great product. Would we have figured this out at another time? I doubt it.

In the middle of this crisis, two things happened. First, some of our largest customers began to negotiate multiyear agreements with us in exchange for our concession to leave them on the old price during a new contractual period. However, that wouldn't benefit us at all, so we asked those clients to grow their license agreements with us as part of the agreement and to extend them. The net new revenue from these expanded arrangements would help us meet the lofty goals we had set for 2020, regardless of what happened with our new client pipeline. The second thing that happened is that clients who entered the pipeline later in the year began to make it clear to us that we had now correctly set our pricing.

Because we were slightly more expensive than lesser competitors (whereas we had previously been underpriced even though we offered better capabilities), our prospects now wanted to dig in and understand what they would receive in exchange for this higher price. This caused them to appreciate our higher value. Our pipeline began to rebuild with high quality, high profile, and higher dollar opportunities.

### The flywheel

Motors and machinery typically use heavy fixed flywheels. The inertia of these heavy flywheels is employed for a variety of purposes. The downside to incorporating a flywheel into a piece of machinery is that it takes more energy to get that motor or equipment up to operating speed due to its weight. However, once inertia is established, it enables consistent force to be applied despite most motors' inconsistent output.

The effort we put into building our businesses, chasing our dreams, or focusing on the thing we believe we can be great at is like putting momentum into the flywheel of our life. The "flywheel" of what has been accomplished in the past can carry us through unexpected short-term difficulties. The work that you have done in the past to build your business and the skills required to run it can get you through an unexpected downturn or a difficulty—if you'll only stay the course.

A loss of focus in either difficult or successful times can do damage to a business. Suppose we react to market changes or opportunities by completely reinventing what we do. This can be the business equivalent of abandoning the momentum of our business flywheel. We can lose the credibility or momentum we have built through past focus; instead, we trade it in for an uphill climb of getting something brand new started, and at the same time, no one is focused on keeping our flywheel spinning at top speed.

This is a maxim and not a universal truth. There are times when it is better to start over than to continue something unfruitful. Far more often, though, we would be wise to continue putting incremental energy into what we already have moving. Unfortunately, this is not the default for human nature. We are not naturally brave when it appears we are about to fall. I think many of us underestimate the power we have stored up in the momentum of our past efforts and fail to leverage our skills, experience, credibility, and goodwill toward "getting through." Most of us will address only the things we do poorly when outside pressure forces us to confront them. Since that pressure is inevitable, our response is better invested in fighting to regain, maintain, or increase our momentum than in trying to start a new project.

**It takes hard work**

Work is not always fun. However, it can be fun when adrenaline keeps you going. There is also satisfaction in knowing that you did whatever it took to make things right. I'm a big advocate of hard work because I've seen firsthand that's what it generally takes to capture opportunities.

I believe the ingredients for extraordinary success are:

1. Identifying a problem or need in the marketplace.
2. Working hard at producing a solution or a better solution for that problem or need.
3. Delivering the product or service at a fair price with high integrity, high quality, high consistency, and hopefully, a high-profit margin! (Remember, if you are not making a profit, you're not actually in business.)

So let me take a moment to discuss what it took to go from being a business owner in a non-technical field to one in a technical field. I didn't see what was happening in the computer industry through some grand vision; I stumbled into it through my own need. I was an entrepreneur first and learned how to be a businessman later. Thank God I continued working hard, or I would never have overcome my shortcomings to make it to the end of all these lessons.

*The peculiarity of the entrepreneur*

The entrepreneurial personality is generally crazy or just peculiar. It's not that we build to accomplish something; the only way we know how to accomplish anything is to create. We have a drive inside that pushes us. It's the faith that "I've got this!" But the journey between dream and accomplishment is never as easy as we hope. Yet, there has never been a better time for entrepreneurs than the present, regardless of when you read this.

If someone like me can persist in achieving something significant, so can you. God has designed each one of us for something meaningful. We might travel through the "desert" first, but perseverance (which will probably include failure, heartache, fear, and most assuredly personal doubts) can eventually get us to a place where we can achieve something that makes a difference in the world, something most are unwilling or unable to dream.

---

### Birth of an Icon: The Story of WD-40

As related in *Today's Machining World Archives*, September 2006, Volume 02, Issue 09

The aerospace industry was centered in southern California in the late 1940s and early 1950s. There was land for big buildings for what were presumed to be huge planes and missiles, and the weather was good year-round to attract employees. The problem was that when aerospace companies built their plants too close to the ocean, the damp air started to corrode the parts of the new planes and missiles.

The new industry not only attracted pilots, factory workers, and marketing folks, it also attracted dreamers and inventors willing to solve these kinds of problems. Three of those research types at the San Diego Rocket Chemical Company came up with a formula in 1953 that they thought would inhibit such corrosion. They

---

had tried 39 times to find a solvent that would both degrease those parts and then provide a rust inhibitor that would stand up to that damp ocean air.

On the 40th try, the water displacement solvent did what it was supposed to do: ergo, WD, as in "water displacement," and 40, as in "the 40th try." It was like Chanel's famous No. 5. No one cares what the first four were, just like no one in the machine industry—or in any of those 80% of American households—gives a hoot about the first 39 formulas. "Everyone, I think, is just happy the researchers didn't give up at, say, 25," said company marketing guru Lesmeister. "It is one of the world's great products."

The first big contractor to use the product was Convair (later a division of General Dynamics Corp.), which was making the Atlas missile. Eventually, Convair's employees discovered the wonders of WD-40 for personal use. They started spiriting the cans home from the plant. They found out it could do, well, almost anything. They could clean and protect their tools with it and could lubricate their lawnmowers and their new suburban kitchen items, too.

In 1958, the bosses at Rocket found out about the in-house smuggling at Convair and decided to make lemonade out of lemons. They put WD-40 in aerosol cans and hired a few salespeople to get it into local hardware stores. By 1960, they were selling 45 cases of the stuff a day. When Hurricane Carla hit the Gulf of Mexico coast, contractors from Texas to the Florida Panhandle had heard of this semi-miracle product. The cult had finally spread east, and through the 1960s, the aerosol can with the funny name became ubiquitous.

By 1969, with only one product, the Rocket Chemical Company officially became the WD-40 Company.

More than one million cans of WD-40 are sold each year, and annual revenues top $150 million. Adding to its mystique is the secret nature of WD-40's formula.

The company owns other products such as 2000 Flushes®, the X-14® cleaner line, the Lava® line, and 3-In-One® dry lube. Still, the bulk of the business, and the fun, comes from WD-40.

The WD-40 Fan Club came about, according to Lesmeister, after people started emailing oddball uses for the product. Now the company website lists more than 2,000 uses for WD-40, from the mundane and predictable ("Keeps garden tools rust-free"), to the sensual ("Loosens crud around stoppers on antique perfume bottles") to the just plain nutty ("Removes stains left from Silly String").

Recently, the company has decided to branch out just a little bit in getting WD-40 in cracks and crevices that had eluded it. There is a new super-sized can, the 18-ounce Big Blast, mostly for big machine shop or automotive bay use. On the other end, there is the WD-40 No-Mess Pen, a felt-tip marker-like dispenser for tight applications.

"We got it out this way to people who hadn't used it before, specifically women, and into crafts and hobby shops and places like Office Depot, another vehicle for distribution," said Lesmeister. "I guess the motto here is we won't rest until everyone is using WD-40, for something, all at once," he said with a chuckle. "It may not be so far-fetched."

**Survival is a precursor to success**

We all have our reasons for being willing to go through whatever it takes to survive. For me, it was the complete and total lack of other options that kept me highly motivated. If you're going to invest in somebody else's startup company, I'd suggest you look for that. If they say, "If things don't work out, I can always go to work with my aunt. She has this great healthcare business." That's not to say that having resources and the ability to recover is a negative, but an "I'll give it my best" attitude, and if it doesn't work out, I can always "fill in the blank" shouldn't be good enough for you if they are going to be spending your money on Plan A, at least not if it's their first time around the entrepreneurial block.

I had no other options, and I didn't even know it. As I already shared, I probably should have been better prepared. The only real asset I had was a strong work ethic, and thank God I had that. I admit fear was a big motivator, and it kept me working hard. In the early years of my first tech business, I had a lot of days and nights, as my wife would attest, that I would go into the office at seven o'clock in the morning then come home at 9 or 10 P.M., get the kids into bed (sometimes), and then I'd go right back to work. I had a Lazy Boy–style chair, and I'd sit in it with a laptop and work until three or four o'clock in the morning. I'd often fall asleep in that chair and then get up at 6:00 in the morning, get into the shower, and be back at the office at seven. I didn't want to work that way, but I didn't have a choice. I had committed to starting the business. I had signed the lease for an office. I had hired staff. I had taken loans from the bank. And if I wanted to survive, I had to do whatever it took.

Learn to delegate early, if you can. But be prepared that there *will* be times, probably many of them, when you'll have to work in ways never expected of people with a "regular job."

There were times when people would come into the office and find that I'd been there all night. It wasn't because I was trying to get people to notice how hard I was working. I'm not trying to impress you with how hard I could work (back then); I'm just indicating that survival has a cost. In real life, you may often feel scared to death, exhausted, and alone.

The truth is that hard work does not guarantee survival. However, there are many situations where the perils we face can be overcome, and we must face the day even when we are unsure how to make it through. We owe it to ourselves to continue working on every available option as diligently as we can.

### What to do if you are already in crisis

If you don't survive, you can't succeed. That's obvious, but it's also important to remember this when you start your business, because there will most certainly be times when your survival is in question. Just as important as a great marketing strategy, a great hiring strategy, and having a valuable commodity in a great market, perhaps more significant than all of these is the determination to survive. If your resources have already been depleted, please go back and read Lesson #3.

If you are in a situation because you have committed yourself to an unworkable business model, consider Winston Churchill's famous quote: "When it is obvious that you are going in the wrong direction, the most progressive is the one who turns around soonest." Sometimes the way forward is to stop going in the wrong direction, but if in your heart you believe your business model can work, do whatever you need to do to get yourself back in a frame of mind to get things done (including taking a break, within limits).

Sometimes, under that kind of pressure, I would innovate the way we did business, reinvent the terminology we used to describe how we delivered value, or re-package offerings in a new way so it was easier for our customers to understand. If everything had been easy, I never would have gotten that done. I would've just kept pressing the button that opened the register so that I could put their money in, give them their change, and close it again. But when existential risk came and I was forced to make things better, I would have to lay down building blocks upon which success was later built.

### A fate worse than failure

But let's cover the alternative. It's okay to fail! It's actually more than okay to fail if you get into business and it doesn't work out. If I were going to hire someone to help me build a new division or practice, I would rather hire somebody who ran a business and failed than hire somebody who never tried. I know that people learn a lot from that, and the experience is priceless. It leads to an understanding that cannot be gained any other way. So it's okay to fail.

### *What's worse than failure is being stuck!*

What's worse than failure is being stuck! I spent five years going sideways when the company was bleeding money one month, making half of it back the next month, and perhaps having a rare good month once a quarter. But then, we'd have to pay the IRS more than we made in profit, and we'd watch the balance sheet (the precarious balance, in our case, between cash and debts) get worse while we fell further behind with creditors every month.

You're going to find yourself in many situations, if you launch a business or if you take on a critical endeavor, where it's going to feel as if you've got no way out. But there is always a way out. It's almost always through perseverance and growth. You are going to need "your best you" to get this done.

**Keep investing in yourself, even in a crisis**

The you that goes into the tunnel isn't the one who will make it out. If you are in a bad situation, buckle up, read Lessons 1 and 2, and start asking for help. Don't go it alone! Seek good counsel.

*Building things is what entrepreneurs do, and it's hard*

When you try to accomplish anything substantive in life, you're going to struggle at some point. That's probably the one thing you can count on. You can have the best plans. You can invest appropriately. You can get the right team together. Yet there's no guarantee that you will ultimately succeed. Certainly, there is no guarantee that you will make it to your goal unscathed. However, if you learn to ask for help and counsel and grow, you may survive and wind up better for the struggle.

I think what leads most of us to become entrepreneurs is the unwavering belief of "I can do this," a belief in self. Maybe you've had it since you were a child. It burns inside some of us like a fire that just can't be quenched except through the joy of success or the bitter finality of failure. Some of us have a particular idea. Some of us watch somebody else do something and believe it can be done better, and we are willing to take the chance.

On October 29, 1941, Prime Minister Winston Churchill addressed his alma mater Harrow School, immortalizing one of his most famous and often misquoted quotes:

"Never give in. Never give in. Never, never, never, never—in nothing, great or small, large or petty—never give in, except to convictions of honor and good sense. Never yield to force. Never yield to the apparently overwhelming might of the enemy." This quote will hopefully embolden you, encourage you, and strengthen you as it did for the Brits and their allies as they fought one of the gravest evils to darken the steps of mankind.

> *He says the best way out is always through.*
> *And I can agree to that, or in so far*
> *As that I can see no way out but through.*

> *—Robert Frost from "A Servant to Servants"*

# THE STEPS TO YOUR OWN TURNAROUND

**#1. Know thyself!**

People who rely on their strengths to an extreme, yet lack the self-awareness required to see their weaknesses, tend to allow their strengths to *become* weaknesses. I was told that I was exceptionally good at giving pep talks. Another one of my strengths was the ability to recover quickly and get back to work with a fury. I assumed everyone was like me, so I expected the same behavior from my people. I would give them a pep talk. At first, this yielded success, but over time, the results reversed. I didn't realize that one of my weaknesses was the inability to empathize with people who had different strengths than I, and so I would rely on my strengths over and over again until they became my enemy. People with different strengths must be allowed to complement and support you while you reserve your strengths for the areas where they are best used.

**#2. Don't go it alone!**

I wish I had learned much sooner how critically important it is to have qualified, trustworthy, and wise counsel available. Finding people you can trust, with whom you can share your challenges and who can understand the challenges you face, is so critical that I would advise my youngest entrepreneurial self to seek out this resource on day one. True leaders gladly mentor the people around them, and wise individuals ask for help. Building trusted advisor relationships requires transparency, so don't fake it. To effectively gain support requires admitting you need it.

### #3. Invest in yourself

In his book *Good to Great*, Jim Collins wrote about "the window versus the mirror." If you asked me why I was having difficulty, I would look out the window and point to all "those circumstances" impeding my way. I did not begin to change until I began to recognize that the cause of my circumstance could be found in the mirror. I would not find real success until I was willing to admit that I was the impediment. Once I accepted that difficult truth, it made sense for me to begin working on myself. If you are going to lead, you may find yourself in circumstances and situations for which you are not prepared. Taking the time to learn about how others have navigated the challenges and opportunities that inevitably come with leadership is how you invest in yourself. The best time to study the writings of other great leaders is yesterday, the second best time is today.

### #4. Be humble

Seeking good counsel isn't possible until you can first accept that others may know better than you. That is at the root of humility. Humility is a super weapon that can disarm those who oppose you, endear halfhearted customers, and inspire others, but like a mythical weapon of old it can be wielded only by the authentic of heart. That is why I didn't say *act* humbly; rather, you have to learn to *be* humble. Humility grows best within the safety of an organization full of people who see themselves as less than perfect but who are improving together, and you must foster that. Suppose we are overly proud of what we accomplished yesterday yet lack the perspective of what we must still accomplish to become our better selves tomorrow. Let's arrive at each plateau with the humility that recognizes we have been given a break and a moment to acknowledge our incomplete progress.

### #5. Prepare for the unexpected

Prepare for the inevitable arrival of the unexpected and factor it in. What about a market downturn? What about the tourist season that doesn't come? Or the new competitor with a feature you don't have? What about the big competitor who announces they are entering your marketplace or the bank deciding they are no longer interested in your industry? Should you be surprised when your largest customer tells you they have been acquired or that your favorite customer chooses to switch to one of your competitors? What about when your best employee starts a competing business and takes half of your top talent? Are you prepared for the public embarrassment of a highly visible error? If one or more of these things has not happened to you yet, let me assure you they will. I know this from experience. The company that expects the unexpected will set aside the resources necessary to press on when it arrives. The unexpected can even bring opportunity.

### #6. The right amount of cash is more

Honest investors and bankers will tell you that they are more comfortable with someone asking to borrow $1.2 million for a one-million-dollar project than they are with someone asking for $800,000. This is true even if they think the borrower might find a way to get the project completed when things go wrong. Someone once asked me for a mathematical formula to figure out what additional resources might be required to do something. My answer wasn't specific, but it was accurate: "Whatever you think you need; you will need more. Probably, a lot more!"

### #7. Learn about non-traditional lenders

Many business owners are unaware of secondary lending markets. I'm not talking about Uncle Louie or the guys who break legs if a payment is missed. I'm talking about non-traditional lenders that loan money for higher-risk opportunities. Of course, they will charge double the interest that banks would, but that also means they can afford a failure rate twice as high. Like banks, they are still spread margin lenders. If you are in crisis and doubt your ability to get through, do not take their money. Don't take a traditional bank's money. Don't take Aunt Sally's money. Don't cash in your retirement account. The sick feeling in your gut is not to be ignored! However, if you are convinced you can survive by adding additional resources, then get over your *Wall Street Journal* rate-reading preconceptions and take a higher interest rate loan.

### #8. Make it easy to buy!

Some entrepreneurs come to the game with sales experience. Some entrepreneurs have backgrounds in training and marketing. I learned it all by trial and error, and I painfully learned that most of what we offer to each other is too complicated. When we figure out how to make the complex simple by packaging, we make it easier for people to buy. None of us wants to know how the latest gadget works; we want to know it will be easy to use and how much it will cost. We'll read the manual after we make the emotional decision to buy. By putting things into neat packages, we are not reducing the offering's value; we are reducing the complexity of buying it. If you don't want your customers to go to your competitors for options, give them options.

Create a stripped-down version for the entry-level buyer and a fully loaded version for the "I want it all" buyer.

### #9. Learn to say no!

"No" will make you money. Some customers have the potential of becoming great customers, but only if you're willing to stand up for yourself when they are not acting like customers at all. Remember, while it may not be easy to get payment from a demanding customer with the highest expectations, that customer may also be quite happy to pay you well if you can deliver while treating him like a great customer. However, when someone asks for terms that turn you into a bondservant, a flunky, or a sucker, remember this: *"No" will make you money!*

### #10. Teach them to do the things you love to do

If you recruit great people to do the things you hate doing, you will inspire them to hate doing them as much as you do. Then they will work hard to prove that you should promote them out of doing those things. Why not skip the frustration of having a team full of people hoping to be promoted out of what you need them to do and bring everyone in to learn some part of your job that you love to do? Then take the role of coach (not judge) so that you can continue inspiring them to be successful and grow. And by the way, they'll be happy to pick up the things you hate doing as well, because you will have inspired them to care about what they do along the way.

### #11. Make incremental improvements NOW

If you study what originally made McDonald's successful, you'll discover that it was a relentless pursuit of small, incremental, time-saving changes. As early adopter banks went fully online, their competitors were suddenly under pressure to compete. We've all seen these kinds of groundbreaking changes. Still, we don't often realize that they are not a "Big Bang," but rather the final emergence of hundreds or thousands of small, incremental improvements that led to the organization suddenly being able to do what others thought was impossible. When you walk into your office, straighten it up. When you hire someone to work in your warehouse, insist that he keeps the work area clean and well organized. When you hire someone to send out your invoices, give him the freedom to calculate how long it takes to get the invoices into the envelopes and determine whether it would be worth buying a machine that could automatically fold the invoices or look into delivering them electronically. I don't mean to suggest that you should micro-manage innovation, but you should demand that micro-innovation is always taking place. These small, incremental improvements will accumulate until your business can also suddenly deliver smooth operations that your competitors cannot. The real goal is to get your people to think constantly about making your service and offerings better.

### #12. Focus on profitable customers

Without customers, all you have is a hobby. Without profitable customers, all you have is a delusion. If you really want to be in business, you have to find out what real customers want and be willing to provide that. But having a customer or customers who are willing to pay you for something is still not enough. If you don't have customers willing to pay you enough to *produce a profit*, you are not really in business. If you are building a business or hoping to create a new market but have not yet taken the time to figure out if any customers want what you will be offering or want it enough to make you profitable, you are on the wrong course. Otherwise, you are planning and will soon be funding an expensive hobby. A business without profitable customers will not be a business for long.

#### #13. Do not separate growth from stability

Growth first, stability later is a recipe for disaster. Some believe that growth is difficult to achieve, and they are right. However, *stable* growth is much harder to achieve. I have seen companies that have grown through mergers and acquisitions powered by piling up debt and mashing together incompatible teams to produce substantial growth numbers. These kinds of results can excite investors and markets. Still, stable growth comes from building understanding, producing superior offerings, establishing cohesive teams, strengthening trust, and working together to serve the clients you already have while seeking out and meeting the needs of new ones.

#### #14. Learn the difference between healthy and unhealthy fear

The right kind of fear is what keeps you moving. Unhealthy fear can keep you from accomplishments. Fear is the enemy of focus. If you play a list of demoralizing "what-ifs" in your mind each night, you may start to believe them during the day, and it will cause you to hesitate when an opportunity presents itself. You are an entrepreneur, and your brain will use some of your quiet time to assess risks that can lead to fear. However, you must learn to tell the difference between healthy and unhealthy fear. If you process fear in healthy ways, you will pause only long enough to evaluate the circumstances and decide on your next action. Unhealthy fear can cause inaction. Inaction makes us more vulnerable to what we fear, and it invites stagnation. While action does not guarantee that we will not suffer from the unexpected, it does increase our odds of succeeding.

### #15. Sacrifice pride, save your reputation

I remember talking to a friend who had been an accomplished international banker at a prior stage in his career. Now he had followed his passion and bought a local radio station. He told me about the challenge of struggling to pay that radio station's bills as time went on. He had never had challenges of this kind before. He couldn't fathom the idea that people were now calling him to collect and that he didn't have the resources to pay them. Like me, he had become another undercapitalized small businessperson. I encouraged him, but I also told him that his reputation would only suffer if he wasn't transparent.

When you find yourself unable to deliver on commitments, the temptation to hold out hope and believe you can still make it work tomorrow is very high. *You MUST sacrifice your pride to save your reputation, because if you try to keep your pride, you will lose both.* It is never a fun conversation when you tell someone that you may or certainly will let him down, and it will most likely have negative ramifications. However, when you tell someone the truth, you allow him to plan, and you also allow him to give you grace. And when you receive grace, you can come through (on new and more realistic terms) showing your appreciation of that grace while restoring that person's faith in you and building a genuine relationship, the kinds of relationships that a business needs for the long haul. An attorney friend of mine taught me a great deal about running my business, and this key takeaway could be summarized by something he often said: "When things go wrong, disclose early and disclose often."

## #16. Know and defend your corporate culture

Building high-performing teams necessitates building and defending a cohesive culture. Many organizations and leaders fail to take culture seriously enough. I built two companies that shared the same office space for more than a decade. That gave me the unique opportunity to see how differently two teams developed with otherwise equal circumstances and environments. One team was a group of people with great relationships developing expertise in a collaborative environment, and the other team was a group of highly functional experts with dysfunctional relationships. If you want to love what you do, you need to love those with whom you are doing it. Design your culture, if you can, ahead of time. If your culture has already emerged on its own, you must still define and foster it.

## #17. Look up!

Humility isn't humility until we can first see how much larger our Creator and His universe are than we will ever be. I believed I was a "good Christian," but in all honesty, I was just another one of those annoying "I am better than you because I dress nicely and stop cussing on Sunday" kind of fakers that give Christianity such an awful name in many circles. I thought God was a magical power I could wield to get red lights to turn green as I rushed to meetings and to get circumstances to turn in my favor in business and relationships. All I had to do was whisper a hurried prayer to this celestial stranger. I believed there was a good and bad scale, and I had put just enough good on it to outweigh my bad. I was an often nasty, self-centered, thankless, uninspiring man who took more than I gave in almost every situation. Even when I appeared to be giving, I was usually doing it to get. As I had given up the purely evil ways of my youth, which were obvious to all at the time, I was now confident that it would all work out fine for the new and externally improved me. Thank God I did NOT get what I deserved!

### *The fear of God is the beginning of wisdom.*
### *Proverbs 9:10*

It wasn't until the trouble that I describe in this book came—trouble that I could not escape by any means—that I began to think that the universe had somehow turned against me. I came to grips with the idea that the good on my scale was so heavily outweighed by the evil that there was no hope of ever reconciling it all in my favor. I was starting to get a taste of what I deserved, and fearing the idea of that, I finally humbled up and began to call out to God for help instead of magic tricks. Next, I began to read the Bible that I had so long claimed to believe. The surprising thing is that so little of what I had believed was in that book. Likewise, many things I had not previously wanted to believe were there. They lept off the pages at me. All of the lessons I have shared in this book came at great personal expense, but they still came at a far lesser cost than Christ paid to reconcile those scales for me. My Savior and friend, Jesus Christ, offered up everything, including His very life. But He gave it freely, all to provide the opportunity for me to come to see the truth, finally humble myself, and recognize what I deserved. The exchange of what I deserved for what He paid is a gift, available to all, just for the asking.

Once I came to know who God is, my eyes were opened, and all the lessons I share from the "edge," over which I deserved to fall, are a credit to my friend Jesus. I looked up. I called out to heaven. I recognized my need, and He rescued me so that I could tell you to look up, too.

*Psalm 121:1–2* ESV:

*I lift up my eyes to the hills.*
*From where does my help come?*
*My help comes from the Lord,*
*who made heaven and earth.*

# ACKNOWLEDGMENTS

Thank God for putting brilliant and wonderful people in my path along the way, even when I failed to appreciate them. Dennis McCallum showed me what it means to lead through developing others. Dave Hendershot gave me the chance to fail up. Ken Gosnell, founder and chief experience officer of CXP, a peer group of Christian CEOs, helped me see that my business's turnaround needed to start with me, and he offered incredibly useful insights as this book came together. My father stood taller than I ever noticed, and my many teammates along the way have helped me accomplish what I would have failed at without their help, especially Carl Casserly and Josh Yeager. The friends and family who took a big risk and invested in me in the early days while I was still wet behind the ears. And a special thanks to Chuck Tressler, who patiently and tirelessly encouraged, supported, and worked with me to accomplish this project. I would also like to thank Al Slade and Roger Franks for their spirited efforts in helping us improve the readability of this book.

# APPENDIX A

# PREPARING A BANKING RFP

You should also prepare a "banking package" that includes:

- A summary letter introducing your company, your management team, why you are seeking a new banking relationship, and what you intend to do with the funds you seek.
- If you can, provide written reference letters from vendors and customers. It is especially helpful if your vendor references can offer specifics about your credit terms, if you have them. Specifics like, "has used credit terms to purchase our goods and services for X years", or "we have increased their credit line 3 times due to good performance with the account", etc.
- A recent copy of your credit report that you have pulled on your own and printed for them.
- A personal financial statement.
  - o There are plenty of Excel templates online into which you can put all the necessary details for a personal financial statement. You must ferociously insist that the bank NEVER pull a copy of your credit report until they have gone through what's called "pre-underwriting." Only let the bank pull your credit report after its underwriter

has done the due diligence and believes they can offer you something you are interested in.

- Include a detailed list of questions about the candidate bank, such as:
    o How long has your bank been in business?
    o Who owns the bank?
    o What are the banks current reserve levels?
    o Who makes lending decisions?
        • Are they made locally or by someone with whom you will have no relationship?
    o Do they offer online banking?
    o Do they offer remote deposits, without fees?
o Do they have couriers?
o What is their typical loan approval rate?
o What sectors of the marketplace do they favor?

Ask them for of all these things and more in writing.

# APPENDIX B

# KEY INVESTMENT TERMS

A few key terms to consider if you approach institutional investors:

- **Stock class.** If you have set up a corporation and issued stock but have not yet taken on institutional investors, you will probably deal mainly in common stock. You may have voting stock, nonvoting stock, and restricted stock within that pool, but you have probably not yet had to deal with preferred stock. Preferred stock is preferred because it will typically include various terms that common shareholders do not have, and I will explain a few of these below.
- **Liquidation preference.** A liquidation preference can have many sub-terms, but in its simplest form, it merely states that if the company is sold, the preferred stockholders will get some, all, or a certain multiple amount of their money back before the stock is divided per share.
- **Drag along rights.** This allows preferred stockholders to "drag along" the common stockholders if they find a potential buyer for the company, assuring them that they will not get stuck in an investment in which other stockholders prefer to camp out and collect dividends or paychecks.

– **Redemption.** This is a failsafe to assure that if no successful exit has been reached by a specific time, the preferred shareholders can assert their right to a preferential buyout plan, which is preconfigured under the title redemption.

– **Dividends.** Remember, institutional investors have typically had to agree to pay their institutional investors a dividend, regardless of what's happening to the companies in their investment portfolio. These dividends often accrue over time as opposed to being paid out along the way. Investors will typically seek the same or higher dividends from you to assure they do not cut into their profits.

– **Board seats and observation rights.** Some investors will insist on a board seat. Some investors will require control of the board. Some investors will want only observation rights, meaning having someone present whenever the board meets.

– **Pre-money.** This is the valuation the investor places on your company before the investment takes place.

– **Post-money.** This is the valuation the investor places on your company after the acquisition takes place.

– **Cap table.** This is a common phrase used to describe the literal spreadsheet showing who owns what percentage of the company. This is important to understand when taking on an institutional investor.

CPSIA information can be obtained
at www.ICGtesting.com
Printed in the USA
LVHW050713060722
722843LV00004B/556